The Old Guard

The Old Guard

Mieczysław Lurczyński

Translated from the Polish by
Alicia Nitecki

Edited and adapted by
Gerald W. Speca

ee

excelsior editions

State University of New York Press
Albany, New York

Published by
State University of New York Press, Albany

© 2010 State University of New York

Originally published in Polish as *Stara Gwardia* (1946). Copyright © The Polish Library, Polish Social and Cultural Association Ltd, 238–246 King Street, London W6 0RF.

Introduction, English translation, and adaptation by Alicia Nitecki and Gerald Speca copyright © 2010 State University of New York.
Printed in the United States of America

For information, contact State University of New York Press, Albany, NY
www.sunypress.edu

Production by Kelli W. LeRoux
Marketing by Fran Keneston

Library of Congress Cataloging-in-Publication Data

Lurczyński, Mieczysław.
  [Stara gwardia. English]
The old guard / Mieczysław Lurczyński ; translated from the Polish by Alicia Nitecki ; edited and adapted by Gerald W. Speca.
    p. cm.
  Originally published in 1946 as Stara gwardia, re-issued in 1971 in slightly abridged form under the title Alte Garde in author's Trzy sztuki (Three plays).
  Includes bibliographical references and index.
  ISBN 978-1-4384-3081-2 (hardcover : alk. paper)
  ISBN 978-1-4384-3082-9 (pbk. : alk. paper)
  1. Buchenwald (Concentration camp)—Drama. 2. World War, 1939–1945—Concentration camps—Drama. 3. Holocaust, Jewish (1939–1945)—Drama. I. Nitecki, Alicia, 1942– II. Speca, Gerald W. III. Lurczyński, Mieczysław. Alte Garde. English IV. Title.

PG7171.U7S7313 2010
891.8'527—dc22   2009026319

10 9 8 7 6 5 4 3 2 1

Introduction

Mieczysław Lurczyński's play, *Stara gwardia* [*The Old Guard*], written in Hanover in 1945 and published by him there in 1946 in an edition of 200 copies, is of value not only because it is an early work of concentration camp literature, but, also because the circumstances under which it came into being are highly distinctive.

The play is based on situations its author had witnessed, characters he had seen, and conversations which he had noted down verbatim on scraps of paper in Buchenwald and its sub-camp, SS-Kommando Hecht, and had miraculously managed to smuggle out of the camps with him. Today, these notes are preserved in POSK, the Polish Library in London. The play was reissued in 1971 in a slightly abridged form under the title *Alte Garde* (German for "Old Guard") in his book, *Trzy Sztuki* [*Three Plays*] by the Oficyna Poetow i Malarzy [Poets and Painters Publishing House] in London.

Lurczyński was born on 14 December 1908, in St. Petersburg to middle-class Polish parents—his father was an office clerk, who had been deported to Russia in 1905 at the end of the Polish revolution. The family returned to Warsaw in 1909. He received a diploma from the Warsaw gimnazjum and a degree from the Academy of Political Science. He then went on to study art at the Warsaw Academy. From 1930 to 1939 his paintings were exhibited in various galleries in Poland, the prestigious Zacheta Gallery among them. During that same period, he began writing poetry. A cycle of poems, *Judasz* [*Judas*] was published in 1937, and a second short volume entitled *Pieśni Buntownicze* [*Songs of Rebellion*] in 1938.

Under the German Occupation of Poland, Lurczyński became a member of the Polish Home Army operating under the name Jan

Kozłowski. When the building in which he was living came under German surveillance, he sought refuge for a few weeks with Halina Martin who hid Jews, Freemasons, and others on her estate in Pawlowice near Warsaw. She remembers him spending his days there, "painting in the open air, and on rainy days finding himself a model for a portrait. In the evenings, he would spread papers out under the oil lamp in the empty dining room and write." He also helped to organize clandestine poetry readings there by various well-known poets including Czesław Miłosz and Leopold Staff. On such evenings, Lurczyński recalls in an essay entitled, "Pawlowice Evenings, or Athens near Warsaw," which he wrote long after the war for Halina Martin, the beauty of the words was such "that for a moment one forgot about tomorrow's threat, about betrayal lurking close by, about the ever-present Gestapo."

On 13 February, 1943, not long after returning from Pawlowice to Warsaw, Lurczyński was arrested. He had possibly been set up. He explains in his 1988 memoir, *Reszta jest milczeniem* [*The Rest is Silence*] that he had received instructions to meet on the evening of 12 February, "a German engineer from the Ruhr who was just then passing through Warsaw. This engineer was apparently an avowed opponent of Hitler's policies. I was to find out from him the truth about the bombing of the Ruhr, about the actual state of German productive capability." The person he was to meet failed to show up, and when Lurczyński called to report this, he was informed that the meeting had been rescheduled for the following day. Shortly after he arrived at the appointed place, the Gestapo came.

He was in Pawiak Prison for a little more than a month, and in mid-March of 1943 he was transported to Majdanek, and from there, a week later, to Buchenwald where he arrived on April 3, prisoner #12243.

In his first months in Buchenwald, he worked in the stone quarry helping to pull heavy metal containers along poorly mounted tracks, and endeavoring whenever he could to get himself assigned to chopping rock with a pick-axe because, "that solitary work allowed me to think," he writes, "and the desire to continue at all cost work which was creative in nature allowed me to compose, to build a sonnet for a collection of poems having nothing to do with Buchenwald."

He was encouraged in these creative endeavors by letters he received from Leopold Staff which assured him that "even though he now found himself in a grave, he was, nonetheless, alive . . . and ordered him to work—work despite everything." Secretly at night in the barracks, he composed on scraps of paper, even on cigarette paper, poems for several such collections, which he hid in a little box with a false bottom. The last one of these, dedicated to Staff, and written, as he says in its preface, to prove to himself that "there existed, and still exists, a different, humane, reality," he left unfinished, because he fell ill, lapsed into indifference, and, on returning to health, became desensitized, "everything going on around me seemed normal now, ordinary, comprehensible."

In the last period of his detention in Buchenwald, perhaps thanks to his friend Prof. Krawczyński whom he had first met in Majdanek and who had been brought on the same transport with him to Buchenwald, Lurczyński was fortunate enough to be assigned to office work in the *Politische Abteilung*. It was here that he began noting down what was happening around him.

On 5 February, 1945, Lurczyński was transported from Buchenwald to SS-Kommando Hecht in Escherhausen, where he officially held the function of *Dolmetscher*, translator, and where, he says in his preface to the second edition of the play, "With my back to the people who were the lords of life and death over all the so-called '*Haeftlingen*' ostensibly immersed in working on the papers of the '*Schreibstube*,' I noted down words, incidents, atmosphere."

When the camp was evacuated at the end of March 1945, and their open-wagoned train was stalled at the station in Celle by Allied strafing, Lurczyński escaped, and made his way to Hanover. There, he cofounded the Publishing Company of the Polish Union of Forcibly Displaced People, immediately publishing through it the pamphlets of poems he had written in Buchenwald; a play he had written, *Jan i Janka*, set on Halina Martin's estate; and his translations into Polish of R. L. Stevenson, Pushkin, and Poe, among other works, some of which he issued under his assumed name, Jan Kozłowski.

In Hanover, he also immediately embarked on his creative work. His art was shown in various towns across Germany, and he was invited by the German Association of Plastic Artists to exhibit his paintings in two exhibitions in Hanover.

On 10 April, 1949, Lurczyński and his wife who had been brought from Warsaw to Hanover by the Red Cross, went to live in Paris, where his art became a collector's item. His postwar poems, plays, fiction, and memoirs were published in London for the Polish émigré community. He died on 29 September, 1992.

The Old Guard is set in SS-Kommando Hecht whose Kommandant, as in the play, was SS Obsturmführer Busch, and where the prisoner hierarchy—Camp Elder, Camp Kapo, Block Elders and Kapos of various Kommandos—were all Polish prisoners, by contrast with Buchenwald main camp where these positions were held by Germans. In that Block Elder's room, the prisoners drank moonshine which they made out of the camp prisoners' store of sugar, and constantly played bridge, "not for money," Lurczyński says, "nor for food, probably just to kill time." A number of the smaller details in the play are similarly based on real people and events: A Jesuit priest, Józef Nowak, did work at the *Schreibstube* in the Camp Elder's room, and did, sometimes, as the priest Głowak does in the play, perform the duties of chaplain accompanying the dead to the common grave; there had been a Jewish prisoner in Hecht named Netter and the Camp Elder did refer to him always as "Judas Maccabeus"; Lurczyński did see a Jewish prisoner coming to ask the Camp Elder for a change of Kommando.

Although in his preface Lurczyński says "in no case do the heroes of the play represent people with whom I met up during my stay in the KZ," the people on whom the two main characters are based are readily identifiable. The passive, decent, but unheroic Kapo who mentions being at a poetry reading on some estate during the Occupation, who had been imprisoned in Pawiak, Majdanek and Buchenwald, and to whom Lurczyński gives the name "Jan," Lurczyński's own assumed name, is based on the author himself. Within the play, Jan, like Lurczyński who in *The Rest is Silence* writes that in Hecht, "I didn't say anything, did not talk about my life, did not share memories of erotic victories, didn't drink, and did not engage in discussion," does not drink, nor reminisce, stays on the periphery of the action, and finds refuge in listening to Fryderyk's anecdotes about his prewar life.

Although he does not explicitly say so, Lurczyński models his main character, the famous actor of the classical stage, Fryderyk, on Fryderyk Jarosy (1890–1960) a theater director, film actor, and renowned king of Warsaw cabaret.

Born in Prague and raised in Vienna, the Austrian citizen Jarosy had come to Warsaw from Berlin with a Russian theater company in 1924, had remained there, and assumed Polish citizenship. Arrested by the Gestapo on 24 October, 1939, for his prewar anti-German activities, imprisoned, brought to trial and convicted in March 1940, Jarosy escaped his guards, and hid in and around Warsaw for four years. He fought in the Warsaw Uprising, and was captured and brought to Buchenwald on 14 August, 1944, where he was registered under his assumed name, Franciszek Nowaczyk.

Instantly recognized as the famous performer he was when he appeared on Block 63 early one morning, some higher-ranking Polish prisoners brought him to Block 37 whose Elder, a friend of Lurczyński's, took him into his room, thereby sparing him from the more gruelling work on a *Zuganger*'s Kommando. On 21 October, 1944 he was transported to Hecht.

Lurczyński spent his evenings in Buchenwald, and subsequently in Hecht, his noontime rest periods with Jarosy: "A conversation with him was an escape," he says in *The Rest is Silence*, "it allowed me to get a breather from the primitiveness and bestiality surrounding me on all sides." And just as Lurczyński was introduced by Jarosy to "the life of a particular section of Warsaw's bohemians from the 'Morskie Oko,' 'Quid Pro Quo,' and other theaters with which Jarosy was involved," so he depicts Jan being drawn into the literary life of Europe by Fryderyk.

A number of biographical details, which Lurczyński gives to Fryderyk, are also based on the real Jarosy. Anna Mieszkowska in her essay about him in *Była sobie piosenka* [*There was a Song*] published in Warsaw, 2006, cites his daughter, Marina Kratochwill, as saying that her father smoked, played bridge, didn't drink, and, more significantly, that her parents had met in the Alps, had stayed at the sanatorium which is the setting of Mann's *The Magic Mountain*, and that her mother was descended from the noted Russian Todleben family—the same biographical details which, in the play, Fryderyk recounts to Jan.

When Lurczyński has Fryderyk express his frustration at not being able to do anything to alter the situation in the Camp Elder's room, and say "Only a few years ago . . . I rejected the pacifying motion of the German court, no matter that it might mean death," he is alluding to an actual situation in Jarosy's life. Brought to trial in March, 1940, Jarosy who could have claimed his Reichsdeutsch citizenship, and who had been offered, for reasons of propaganda, the opportunity of running a theater for the German occupiers of Poland, his daughter says, chose instead to abide by his Polish citizenship.

Most significantly, in his affectionate, epistolary preface to the little pamphlet of Jarosy's wartime anti-German propaganda poems, *Mein Kampf (Walka z Doktorem Goebbelsem)* [*A Battle with Dr. Goebbels*], which he published in Hanover in 1945, Lurczyński says to Jarosy, "In you remained hidden a man of truly European culture, for whom, in many instances, choice was not an option, and who, therefore, did not accept compromise, but proceeded with clarity and precision into open battle with scumbags before whom literally everyone else retreated." It is this aspect of Jarosy's character upon which Lurczyński elaborates, and which, in the play, leads to Fryderyk's death.

Lurczyński takes these situations he had observed, the people amongst whom he had lived, and his own experiences in Buchenwald and Hecht, and weaves them into a play whose focus is on, as he says in the preface, "the methods by which people were turned into beasts, and beasts into freaks of nature." In so doing, the play is ideologically close to another book written at about the same time: Siedlecki, Olszewski, Borowski's *We Were in Auschwitz*, Munich 1946, the work for which Borowski wrote his world famous stories, and what Anatol Girs, himself a former concentration camp prisoner and the inspiration behind, and publisher of, this latter work, said about it in his preface applies equally to Mieczysław Lurczyński's play:

> This book is a modest fragment of a story about the life that millions of Europeans lived until not so long ago. Perhaps it doesn't have any great artistic value. But its documentary worth is indisputable, because this book portraying the pathological changes in the soul of these Europeans, is an eloquent testimony to the fact that one of the worst of human crimes is that of striking out the fundamental ethical principle that 'God created man free.'

Alicia Nitecki

Preface

The impetus behind this book set in a concentration camp was my personal need to come to grips with the truth. Everything in it is, or at least endeavors to be, faithful to the truth—language, action and atmosphere. A truth, however, that does not encompass one or another incident, which could have happened at almost any time and in any surroundings, but a synthesizing truth which could be seen as an algebraic symbol solving an equation, transforming an unknown into a self-evident result. In striving to preserve this truth, I forced myself to use a completely alien language, a language which I heard around me over the years. I had the opportunity to note down verbatim and at firsthand many scenes, many phrases, many accounts. Obviously, life in a KZ was far more varied and this play does not subsume the whole because no play in the world would be capable of encompassing it. What was done to people locked up behind wires and dressed in stripes simply defies description. But then, the purpose of this play is not an encyclopedic amassing of facts, just a selection of them to achieve the chosen goal.

In any case, this play does not have great atrocities in it. The focus, rather, is on internal experiences and on depicting pained, sick, desperate, and resigned psyches, on depicting the methods by which people were turned into beasts, and beasts into freaks of nature. The action is rather pale, pale by comparison with that demented flywheel, called a KZ, which day after day seizes thousands of people and throws them into the open jaws of the crematorium, that contemporary invention of Baal's.

The language of this book, the depraved language of a human cesspool, forces me to keep strict control over the entire publishing endeavor. Just as, on the one hand, my firm conviction inclined me to publish the play, so on the other hand, I firmly realize the fact that this book is not intended for the general reader. I am printing it in an edition of 200 copies, and furthermore each copy will be sent by me personally to people who will tolerate the raw breath blowing from its pages, and who will realize the moral imperative of telling the truth, the truth at any price, since truth alone is creative.

Almost without exception, it is Poles who take part in this play. I am, therefore, obliged to state quite definitively that only considerations of a formal nature, a certain simplification of composition, and a concern to make it easier for the reader to assess the aims in writing the play, made me choose a community with which I share the common bond of nationality. National considerations in this play, however, are negligible. And camp experience revealed to me that in all national groups represented in the KZ one could find individuals made degenerate by camp life, and that only among certain minor segments could one distinguish the mentality of an actual criminal or psychopath from eastern and western Europe.

I must also firmly stress that in no case do the heroes of the play represent people with whom I met up during my stay in the KZ. The truth of a work of art, synthesizing and, in a certain sense, defining a higher purpose, has nothing in common with an accidental conglomeration of facts which the author meets up with and passes as he goes on his way. That would be as though stones lying randomly around were to constitute the same value as they do when the patient hand of a mosaic artist lays them on wood in an organized manner.

I do not know how intense the feeling of hatred and outrage toward the author on the part of the readers will be. I think it will be strong, and from many sides at that—above all on the part of former camp companions. Instead of writing in the typical style of martyrdom, instead of exposing wounds, talking only about self-sacrifice and heroism, this book endeavors to bring different matters to light, and aspires to dispel legends. The public's outraged morality will probably also not spare invectives. The fact, however, that I wrote this book in the KZ where it was easy to lose one's head for doing such work, that I managed to carry it out with me during the bombardment of the station at Celle and to hang on to it during my escape across the military fronts obliges me to continue to avail myself not of the smile, but of the Homeric applause, of Fortune.

I dedicate this book to my closest companions together with whom I struggled in the depths of contemporary hell, and above all to:

Prof. Zygmunt Zaleski
Prof. Jan Krawczyński
Prof. Jan Jakubowski

May they accept this book in the spirit in which I wrote it.

Mieczysław Lurczyński

Photograph of Lurczyński in Paris, courtesy of POSK.

Cast of Characters

GENIEK: A sports reporter, yellow journalist. Medium height, broad-shouldered and muscular. He has the style of an ambulance-chaser. Full of vitality, his theatricality masks the true nature of his motives. (Goes for what he can get.) He hides his hopelessness beneath his flights of fancy.

CZESIEK: Another journalist. Tall and thin; he stutters: a clinical accident or mental aberration. His servility is more than likely an inborn character trait. Primitive and literal-minded with flashes of insight and brilliance.

ERNEST: Nobody; and only in this regard is he like Odysseus. He is concerned with peace (and quiet), the ability to play bridge, and his own safety.

FRYDERYK: An old actor of considerable renown; a man of the 19th century: romantic, self-centered, idealistic. He is a relative newcomer who is being 'looked after' in the Camp Elder's Barracks.

JĘDRZEJ: 19 years old. His universities were the concentration camps of Lublin, Auschwitz, Birkenau, Buchenwald; fascinating in his pathology.

GŁOWAK: A priest; a hardened worker at the Schriebstube.

NETTER: The admissions clerk at the hospital.

JEWISH PRISONER 1

KOSTEK: The storekeeper (supply steward).

JAN: A Kapo (foreman) of one of the work units (Kommandos); an intellectual of extensive, exceptional camp experience.

VORARBEITER KOMINEK: Another foreman.

LAGERSCHUTZ 1

VAN DER BOSCH

GÓRECKI

LAGERSCHUTZ 2: JEWISH PRISONER 2

UKRAINIAN PRISONER

PIPEL: A teenager; works for the kapos; whipping boy of the camp.

OTHER LAGERSCHUTZE

SANIN: A Russian tailor.

MARKOWSKI: A Polish tailor.

TWO OTHER TAILORS

DOCTOR: LEICHENTRAGERS

KAZIK

The Setting

The Lageraeltester's room on the Block. On the right, a two-tiered bunk covered with gray blankets. On the left, high up on the wall, a grated, rag-covered window and below it a single bunk temporarily changed with the help of wooden planks into a Schreibstube. In the center of the room, a table. By the table, the Lageraeltester's scruffy armchair. A door to the left of the Schreibstube. The room looks like a junk room in which a stove, cupboards, stools, a few bits of hung-out clothing constitute the most easily identifiable forms. A general sense of chaos, filth, and slovenliness.

Throughout the action of the play, which takes place from late evening to early dawn, sirens distant and near sound anti-aircraft alarms.

Act I

Evening. GENIEK *sits on the armchair, his feet against the legs of the table. The top buttons of his trousers are undone. A cigarette dangles from his mouth as he riffles and studies the cards in his hands. After a moment:*

GENIEK: Clubs, I said.

CZESIEK: P-p-pass. Like from here to M-M-man . . . churia. *(He chuckles.)*

ERNEST: Pass.
(He stretches out his hand and waves smoke from Geniek's cigarette toward his nose trying to inhale the aroma.)

FRYDERYK: Two diamonds.

GENIEK: Three spades.

CZESIEK: Pass.

FRYDERYK: Pass.

ERNEST: Pass.

GENIEK: C'mon, dammit. Play.

CZESIEK: At least Fryderyk says something sometimes. Me, I d-d . . .
(stutters; abandons the idea)
. . . and if I say something, th-then I l-lie without . . . Three.

GENIEK: Three's already been bid! Jesus Christ!
They play a round, throwing cards on the table and picking up discards.

FRYDERYK (*laying a card on the table*): *S'il vous plait.*

CZESIEK (*throws down a card, humming*): Tum ta-dum dee dum. Ta ra ree, ta ra ra

ERNEST (plays a card): We're going to play diamonds . . .

GENIEK (*counts trick*): Three, four.

CZESIEK: Th-th-that's life.

GENIEK: It's the only play, stupid ass. I just said three clubs out of desperation.
The card game continues during the following dialogue.

CZESIEK (*feels the fabric of Geniek's trousers*): Nice. Say, did you organize these from me?

GENIEK: Uh, uh. Most definitely not.

CZESIEK: Oh. B-b-because I had a pair just like them in the storeroom. I remember the color clearly . . .

ERNEST: Pass.

GENIEK: Bullshit. Yesterday, these trousers hung off the ass of some Yid on Block 4, the latest *Zugang*. I dropped in while Heniek was having them processed and I saw this gimpy fucker pulling them off. I liked them as soon as I saw them and told Heniek I had to have them. Today the tailor pressed them and brought them to me.

FRYDERYK: Pass.

CZESIEK: So probably someone else took the ones from my place. Did they give the Jews *Zebrakleidung* because of the latest escapes?

GENIEK: Pass. Of course not. The Hebes never escape. They're fucking cowards. The Russkies, now? They'll break out of here in a heartbeat; but the Jews? They just get their clothes exchanged. And they get searched. All the fucking time. They have what's hard and soft, stuff of value. Hey, look. I saw an opportunity and I took it. Excellent worsted. French . . . military *blau* . . .

CZESIEK: Th-three spades.
Jędrzej slides down from the top bunk and studies Geniek's trousers. He frowns and shakes his head.

JĘDRZEJ: They're stained.

GENIEK: What?

JĘDRZEJ *(pointing to a spot on the trousers)*: See for yourself.
Geniek bends over and rubs the stain vigorously. Jędrzej, with a casual ease, pulls a twist of tobacco from the box on the table next to Geniek and returns to the bunk. Despite his youth, Jędrzej is an experienced Lager thief.

FRYDERYK: Two left the *Steinkommando* yesterday, starving; the day before that, one from Duman. Within two days five people have died on the Revier. And we play bridge.

GENIEK: And what would your rather do, limpdick? Stroke your weenie? Go ahead. Who knows? It might do you some good.

CZESIEK: Old g-gray beard is a decent fellow.

ERNEST: Our only comfort.
Geniek gets up and goes to the Schreibstube. He examines a document and at the same time pulls Głowak's hair.

GENIEK: What hard hair he has! Like pig bristles.

JĘDRZEJ *(drawling)*: Maybe a pig played a part in the black shepherd's conception.

GENIEK: Sure seems that way, doesn't it?
(returning to the card game)

That's ours. An eight . . .
Geniek puts down the tricks and counts them.

FRYDERYK *(quietly intoning)*: The scent of lilacs through the night.

GENIEK: It seems we're short one.
He arranges the cards to count them. Fryderyk rolls a cigarette out of sage and lights it.

GENIEK *(wrinkling his nose)*: Smells like old people.

CZESIEK: D-dirty diapers . . .

ERNEST: Palm Sunday.

GENIEK: No. Chopin's "Funeral March." Pum, pum, pa pum.

CZESIEK: . . . or "In a Dark Grave."

FRYDERYK: I'd rather smoke sage than steal tobacco from other people's parcels.

GENIEK: Not me.

CZESIEK: You're playing like a horse's ass with a s-s-secondary education.

ERNEST: Which he is.

FRYDERYK: I have the one and the other, bridge scum.

GENIEK: Instead of a brain.
Netter, the Schreiber on the Revier, enters with a death announcement and gives it to Głowak.

GENIEK: What's new, Mr. *Schreiber* "Judas Maccabeus" Netter?

NETTER: An announcement. About Ulrich's death.

GENIEK: Ulrich's gone?

NETTER: Yes. A moment ago.
He exits.

JĘDRZEJ: I told him straight away when he came six months ago that he wouldn't get out of here alive. Cocksucker didn't want to offer me any chocolate. Fuck him and the horse he rode in on.

GENIEK *(with irony)*: Evidently the old man was cheap and didn't care to share any of his Red Cross packages.

JĘDRZEJ: He had a lousy last name.

GENIEK: He was a frugal man. Scraped crumbs from his clothes with a toothpick. Did you know he had false teeth?

JĘDRZEJ *(slowly getting off the bunk)*: Really? Now, that has to be dealt with. Before his neighbors get interested.
He slips out of the room.

GENIEK: Any of you birdbrains know how much gold goes into a bridge?
No one responds.

CZESIEK: I guess the game's over. Shall we sing a song?

ERNEST: Don't start fucking around, Czesiek.
Jędrzej returns and sits by Geniek. He reaches behind him, finds a small mirror on the shelf and looks at himself in it, picking at his blackheads, examining his teeth, stretching and picking at his lips. Geniek, looking at his cards, suddenly smacks Jędrzej in the face and knocks the mirror out of his hand and onto the floor.

GENIEK: —And I told the kid not to mess around either.
Jędrzej doesn't react. He shakes his head and smiles.

JĘDRZEJ: I've said more than once that the prick in you would show up sooner or later. *Nicht war?*[1]

---

[1] "Isn't that so?"

(Jędrzej grins broadly, revealing his gums.)
A moment of silence. A Jewish prisoner in terribly torn, stained prison stripes comes into the room and takes off his hat.

JEW: I wish to ask Mr. *Lageraeltester* for some clothing. Mine is completely ruined.

CZESIEK: And wh-where were you yesterday wh-when the new garments were being distributed?

JEW: Where was I? I don't know where I was. They distributed clothing yesterday?

GENIEK: Give the Abyssinian something.
Czesiek gets up and goes out; the Jew follows him. Jędrzej starts after them, then pauses at the door. He crosses back to the table and takes half the tobacco out of the box Czesiek has left behind, hiding it in his own cigarette case. He sits down nonchalantly on the stoop. He wags his head from side to side smiling.

ERNEST: So, it wasn't worth it to follow Czesiek, organizing?
Geniek takes tissue from his pocket; he and Jędrzej roll a cigarette out of the stolen tobacco.

GENIEK: Jędrzej has great respect for the old Polish adage that a bird in hand is better than looking at jackets at Czesiek's.
Jędrzej lolls his head and grins. He takes a piece of gold out of his pocket and examines it carefully.

JĘDRZEJ: The sonofabitch couldn't afford a bigger bridge, and the gold isn't the best.
He tests the hardness of the gold with his teeth, then stuffs the bridge in his pocket. He crawls onto the bunk, hangs his jacket on the rail, and lies down. He falls asleep instantly.

GENIEK: What's with that fucking *Bloedeaeltester*![2] Czesiek!

---

[2] A disparaging title

CZESIEK (O.S.): In a minute.

GENIEK: Kill the fucking Jew and come play.

CZESIEK (O.S.): S-stop shouting! Głowak'll hear you and a-after the war he'll curse us from the pulpit!
Fryderyk takes a table knife and sharpens the pencil used to keep score during the card game. Geniek snatches the knife away from him and weighs it in his hand. Then he aims at the door with the knife.

GENIEK: First man through that door gets a knife in his belly. What d'you think? Fryderyk. Go stand by the door. Don't be afraid. I'll aim to the side. I won't even graze your eye. You can recite a martyr's song.
Fryderyk shrugs and peers at the cards. Geniek looks around and sees the sleeping Jędrzej. He aims the knife at him.

GENIEK: What's the wager that I get him in the gut?
Geniek throws the knife at Jędrzej, hitting him in the chest and waking him.

JĘDRZEJ *(turning his head lazily)*: It's rather amusing, the way you old farts carry on.

FRYDERYK: You could have wounded him, Geniek!

GENIEK: It's *Arbeitszeit* now, shitheads. Everyone is to work *restlos*. Did you hear that, *Lagerkapo*?
Jędrzej raises himself up and leans his head on his hand.

JĘDRZEJ: Do you have your head up your ass, you old eunuch? Or are you finally going out of your fucking mind?

GENIEK: How dare you speak to the *Lageraeltester* like that? Get off that bunk on the double!!

JĘDRZEJ *(not laughing)*: Very funny.
Geniek gets up from the table.

GENIEK: What, *Missgeburt?*

JĘDRZEJ: It's all very interesting. Głowak, say the prayers for the dead.
Geniek crosses to the bunk.

GENIEK: Now, *du Arschloch, Bloedehund?*

JĘDRZEJ *(in the same position)*: Have you prepared the valerian? The opium? I'll finish you off in two days.

GENIEK: Me?
He rolls up his shirtsleeves and reveals his muscular arms.
There's still grit here, asshole. Off the bunk on the double! I could pick up ten like you with one hand. Old Auschwitz, that's what I am.

JĘDRZEJ *(still unmoving)*: Hey! Me too. Have you got the valerian?
Geniek grabs Jędrzej's arm. They wrestle. An unexpected resistance on the part of the tuberculoid Jędrzej. He fights and clutches stubbornly as Geniek drags him off the bunk. Finally, slipping, he falls to the ground and then sits up gasping and coughing.

GENIEK *(pale and worn)*: I told the little fuck not to get excited.

JĘDRZEJ *(smiling wickedly)*: Have you got the valerian? Or the opium?
(as opposed to Geniek, he quickly recovers)
I'm only twenty years old. I'll finish you off.
Geniek seizes the knife and aims it at Jędrzej, who flinches.

GENIEK: That's what you think. I'll smoke you.
Jędrzej takes the box of Geniek's tobacco and begins to roll a cigarette, slowly and deliberately as usual.

GENIEK: Get to work, shithead!
He hefts the knife. Jędrzej smokes the cigarette, and calmly monitors Geniek's movement. Czesiek enters.

CZESIEK: I used to th-throw the knife like this—
(He demonstrates.)

GENIEK: Stand by the door, Jędrzej. We're going to throw at you.
*Jędrzej, still smoking, leans against the door and deftly defends himself
against the knives thrown at him.*

JĘDRZEJ: What's the matter with you douche bags? Why don't you
go buy some paper shields and toy arrows. This shit isn't funny.
(He frowns and nods seriously.)

GENIEK *(warming to the game)*: I'm telling you, Jędrzej, stay by the
goddamned door!
*Jędrzej clucks like a chicken and curses, covering up against the items
thrown at him by both men. When they become more insistent, he
ducks behind the door. Each time he tries to come back, he's met by a
new onslaught. Occasionally a knife clatters against the closed door and
falls to the ground.*

GENIEK *(out of breath)*: Get to work, you prick! Is this how you
show respect for the *Lageraeltester*?
*He reaches into Jędrzej's jacket, finds the false teeth, studies them for
a moment, and then puts them in his own pocket. Jędrzej comes back
in. His head is covered with a wire net, topped by a fantastic hat with
an enormous brim. In his hand he holds a pair of rusty tin snips. A
blanket is thrown across his arms and chest. He stands nonchalantly
at the door, waits a moment, then comes to the table. Holding the tin
snips under his arm, he rolls a cigarette out of Geniek's tobacco.*

GENIEK *(throwing the knife on the table)*: One might say that's
quite a knightly outfit you're wearing, young man. You're probably
looking to poke somebody's eyes out with those cutters. Best be
careful you don't pluck out your own at the same time. Come,
gentlemen, let's sit down and play bridge.

GŁOWAK *(from the Schreibstube)*: As usual, it's spring and violets.

GENIEK: Who's dealing?
*Czesiek yanks his shirttails out of his trousers and closely examines the
seams.*

CZESIEK: Oh, shit! Is that a flea?!

GENIEK *(singing)*: "I said flee, flee, flee, my love, and so she fled . . ."

ERNEST: When I was still in Birkenau, I worked in the *Gaertnerei*. After the disinfection was carried out in the women's camp, we were the first to be admitted. Who knows why? The Blocks were still locked, sealed, and gassed. We walked between the barracks, along the path. We were supposed to tidy things up. I'm telling you, the number of fleas I saw was more than you could ever imagine. Must've been billions of them. A carpet of fleas rising and falling before us as we passed. We tied the bottoms of our trouser legs with string, did the same to our shirtsleeves. Nothing helped. In the blink of an eye we were covered with black, moving dots, which you could pick up by the handful. We had bites all over our bodies. We didn't know where to scratch first. And that was just in the *Frauenlager*!

JĘDRZEJ: Oh, fleas aren't shit. The lice among the prisoners-of-war in Auschwitz were a show all by themselves. You could make cutlets out of them. They were huge. Once this starving, half-dead Russian—they got twenty grams of bread a day for their work—reached under his jacket, poked around in his armpit and pressed a heap of lice onto the back of an SS man who was passing by—Man, we hated those fuckers—shortly after that, the SS-man died of typhus.
He imitates the behavior of the Russian, takes the hat and net off his head, lights a cigarette, and climbs onto the bunk. He immediately falls asleep with the cigarette still burning in his hand.
Seeing that Jędrzej has fallen asleep, Geniek yells, hitting his mouth with his hand.

GENIEK: Eee . . . ee . . . eee . . . ee . . .
(throwing the stool to the floor)
Jędrzej!

JĘDRZEJ *(barely opening his eyes)*: What?! You motherfucking sons-of-bitches! Let me sleep, for Christ's sake! You should rot in hell, every fucking one of you!

GENIEK: Ulrich was just here asking about his teeth.
Jędrzej turns on the bunk, reaching his hand into his jacket pocket. He doesn't find the bridge, shakes his head.

JĘDRZEJ *(smiling)*: So that's why you threw me out the room, cocksucking, well-heeled scumbags . . .

GENIEK: So stop organizing from corpses, dicknose.

JĘDRZEJ: "Dicknose" yourself. Better I should organize from a friend?
He turns and falls back to sleep.

FRYDERYK *(mindlessly flipping the cards)*: Listen. We need to think about the holidays. Easter is in two weeks . . .

GENIEK: That's right. Yeast-er is a-comin' . . .

FRYDERYK: . . . we have some ersatz yeast in the cupboard. We'll need flour.

GENIEK: For what?

FRYDERYK: To bake a little white bread that we could substitute for cake.

GENIEK: Why? It won't be any good.

FRYDERYK: Why not? I saw on the package a drawing of a fat cook with a big *babka* on a tray. The ad said *'Kuchen.'*

GENIEK: Who said anything about wanting to bake *'Kuchen'*?

FRYDERYK: What else would we bake?

CZESIEK: Can you believe this penis brain?! What? Are you half kicked in the ass or something?
Kostek knocks, enters with a card in his hand, and crosses to Głowak who is busy at the Schreibstube.

KOSTEK: Can you give me today's camp numbers? I need it to pick up food rations.

GENIEK: When are you measuring out the sugar?

KOSTEK: Today.

GENIEK: You know what I'm thinking?
Kostek studies Geniek for a moment, then makes a gesture as if catching Geniek's thoughts flying through the air.

KOSTEK: I can't organize more than five kilograms from the storeroom. They don't have much there.

GENIEK: I don't give a shit! You need to scrape me off ten, get it?
He rises from the table, takes Kostek by the arm, and leads him to a corner of the room. They talk in whispers. Only the odd word can be heard: 'mash,' 'moonshine,' 'three days.'

CZESIEK: Douche bag, Lager slut!! Sugar won't replace yeast. Jędrzej!

JĘDRZEJ *(waking)*: Stop picking on me, you bald-headed piece of shit. Let me sleep.

CZESIEK: G-go to the third Block. A *Zugang* arrived yesterday. Organize two, three non-Lager shirts. We have to have yeast.

JĘDRZEJ: And what, dumb ass? You don't know how to shove Jews around? You need a fucking surrogate? You're the one with the hard on, so pipe down, asshole, and go do it yourself.
He goes back to sleep. Czesiek crosses to him, pulls his ear, and then leaves the room.

GENIEK *(to Kostek)*: Come on. Let's have a look. We might be able to goose them up a little.
They exit.

ERNEST: So much for a game of bridge. I suppose I could go the *Arbeitsdienstfuehrer* and arrange for the people we'll need tomorrow. I wonder what *Arbeitseinsatz* they'll give.
He gathers the cards, rises from the table, and exits. Fryderyk sits alone at the table, bent over and holding his head in his hands, gloomily silent. JAN enters and gives Głowak the Kommando list.

JAN: Today's work detail.
(crossing to Fryderyk who remains lost in thought)
Fryderyk! What's the good word?

FRYDERYK *(through his teeth)*: All words are shit in this dung heap of human existence.

JAN: Eh? What's the matter?
Fryderyk raises his head, looks blankly at Jan. Suddenly he bangs his fist on the table.

FRYDERYK: I'm such a coward, that's what the matter is! I ought to smash their faces, these conniving lowlifes! It's unthinkable, unfathomable.

JAN: And whose faces are these that we're smashing?

FRYDERYK: Every one of the bastards. For what they do. How they behave. For their tireless degradation of the human spirit. With full awareness . . . and with complete perfidy. With that attitude they learned in the concentration camp—their great academy of depravity. Do you know what they are?

JAN: Fryderyk. Who are you talking about?

FRYDERYK: Them! The *Alte Garde*. I tell you, they're Germans. That's the price they've paid. Otherwise, they'd have gone up the chimney like the rest! But that I, that I acquiesce, that I permit it. Only a few years ago I had the guts to stand up to a guard who spoke rudely to me. I rejected the pacifying motion of the German court, no matter that it might mean death. But today . . . I sit among them in disgrace, with such mortification amid my own people! How they behave . . .

JAN: Fryderyk, you've had the good fortune not to have experienced the force of the Lager until now. You don't know what the horror of that kind of schooling can do.

FRYDERYK: Yes. And I know you endured it. And that is why you have a different standard of judgment. One adapted to the situation. I know that. But that standard can never be mine. I want to look at these horrors as a civilized man should, through the eyes of a man of Western Europe. I don't want to 'understand' anything. Otherwise, after we leave this slaughterhouse, all of us will have to relearn the principles of civilized life. Just think what a big deal we used to make of the slightest insult, a thoughtless remark—whole issues of honor. But today?

JAN: I'm not so sure it was all that good back then. My conscience isn't clear about that. When I think about the stupidity, the lack of ethics, the short-sightedness and irresponsibility there was in prewar Poland . . . And my own preoccupation with building my little fortune maybe just a cut above envying the wealth of others. I mean, I never raised my voice in these matters. I didn't have the guts, apart from feeling an attachment to European culture, to condemn Berez or the political attitude toward Lithuania, to speak out against the partitioning of Czechoslovakia by a nation that was itself partitioned in the eighteenth century. I couldn't afford to raise a cry which would have drawn everyone's attention, a cry which already existed in Orzechówki: "We're dying." So who knows what compromises I will be capable of, and what I will pass over in silence, if I survive the Lager. And I saw all the evils, standing, as I did, far from political affairs. It wasn't so good, Fryderyk. We are not a nation marked by civic courage. Military bravery? Yes.

FRYDERYK: But we have to recognize that this is cowardice, that we can't gain anything by it. That the value, the whole point, of communal existence rests upon individual heroism. Only personal bravery, independence, can raise the norm.

JAN: Yes. That's true. Sometimes. But sometimes a different, more balanced approach seems more correct. Maybe we should call it 'self-defensive cowardice'? I don't know. Some other principle of judgment, a kind of patience, without taking part in the evil that surrounds us, yet without evangelizing or martyrdom, without heroism in the grand style. You know, I was in Majdanek near Lublin with an old German scholar, a Professor Jan Rawczyński, who had been an Austrian officer, a wonderfully wise man and a Pole by birth. He told me how during his interrogation by the local Gestapo he fought with them and did not allow himself to be tortured so long as he had the strength to defend himself. Even when three of them were sitting on him, he still managed to bite one of them on the hand. Others told me that he was brought to the cell at the Castle a lump of bloody flesh with broken ribs and damaged lungs. A mess. Yet, thanks to his iron resolve he remained alive. Recently, when I was in Buchenwald, I worked with him in the *Politische Abteilung*. Our whole Kommando returned to the Lager for lunch. He led, walking by the side of the division. And some SS man, walking opposite, without cause, just out of ill-humor, punched him in the face. Simple as that. Punched this old man. I was even more amazed, however, by Rawczyński's reaction. He, who in Lublin would not allow himself to be touched, walked quietly by the SS man, continuing to lead his Kommando. He did not react at all. He didn't throw up his fists, he didn't curse, didn't blush; his facial expression didn't change. It was as though nothing had happened. Quietly, he walked next to his Kommando, every now and again smiling and cracking a joke. And he felt that blow without question. The *Politische Abteilung* was the aristocracy of the Lager and it was the custom that these people were no longer beaten. But, you see, Rawczyński knew two ways of behaving, and he chose the second way this time, a different kind of heroism, some other sense of dignity and strength. And I saw how he walked that road, without preaching, without trying to change the world, without railing about human harm, which he undoubtedly saw and felt. I owe him a great deal. My life. He stole my papers, which had arrived from Poland, out of the *Politische Abteilung*, exposing himself, of course, to great danger.

FRYDERYK: But . . . it's revolting. It's a Lager-enslavement mentality.

JAN: You could be right. But, had I not found that umbrella, I would have died the first day I was in the Lager, standing up to defend a man who was being whipped to death in front of me; or when a muscular Kapo—a Jew, no less!—beat me on the head and back with a plank he tore from a fence; or earlier in Pawiak when the Ukrainians taunted us with whips as we made our daily march to the toilet. Maybe I'm wrong, but in the Lager it's already a big deal if you harm no one, and, as far as you are able, help with a word of encouragement or a piece of bread.

FRYDERYK: I can't reconcile myself to this way of thinking. I'm too old . . .

JAN: No. You're simply still rebelling. You have thin skin. And around here one has to wear armor that nothing can penetrate. The armor of quiet dignity. In a few months you'll learn to look and not see, to listen and not hear, to help but not react. But more important, you'll find the goodwill to understand those who went through the daily horror of death and hunger and humiliation, whose psyches were dismantled and broken. These are severely damaged, unhappy human beings . . . And, if they still have an occasional impulse, some true grasp of their own situation, even that turns against them because it drives them to drunkenness and debauchery and speeds up their decline.
(beat)
Look, I could be wrong. But in camp you're doing something important if you can avoid hurting somebody else.

FRYDERYK *(wringing his hands)*: But how can anyone maintain his self-respect among so much shit? All I see around me are jackals gnawing at the bones of the dead and the near dead. I can't coexist with them, can't find a tone which wouldn't sound false. Yet I've had a life rich with relationships and conflict. Do you know that in Munich I was one of the founders of the German *"Jugendstil"* movement? That I lived for a time with Kellermann, talked with Wedekind, met with Rilke? Do you remember Kellermann's "Ingeborg"? That little story in it about the stars? How on one particular night the stars fell to earth and people discovered that there was nothing beautiful or great about them? How they cursed the priests and the prophets who had encouraged them to pray to something that was simply a piece of gilded cardboard? And how one of the scorned prophets, looking up to the sky, saw there one single, lonely golden star shining mysteriously? How he shouted to the people who were jeering him: "It doesn't matter that there are so many fallen stars, since that one in the sky is shining so full of splendor." Do you know that I was the author of that story? An unwitting author, like many of us during one of Lili Nevinna's soirées. And that I, who told people to believe even if only one star was shining in the sky, cannot myself, today, see that star? It's been hidden from me by this trash, by these vermin who exhale some kind of poisoned air that ravages beauty and art, who have the power to devastate a life that hopes for more than pouncing on a victim or tearing at carcasses and bones.

JAN: You never told me . . .

FRYDERYK: Whatever for? Tell you that I created the environment out of which emerged the wild murmuring of Morgenstern? Or that I posed for Stuck and was his young friend? So that today, any sonofabitch,
(pounds his fist on the table)
any good-for-nothing, can lord it over me for the price of this bunk in which I can't sleep,
(points to the Schreibstube on the bunk)
for the price of a slightly better bowl of soup . . . for the fact that, as a result, I have the right to live a few days longer without lice and without increasing filth?

JAN: Fryderyk, you need to calm down a little.

FRYDERYK: Calm down?! Do you realize that after the war I could be named a collaborator? That each one of these criminals will be able to identify me as a friend who sanctioned his deeds? Attest that I not only consented by my silence but in fact took part in all that they did here? My God! Every piece of meat and bread in this place stinks of theft! Did you know that Jędrzej organized a search on the Block and robbed every one of the newly-arrived Jews? Do you realize that he takes those stolen things out of camp and buys cigarettes, vodka, and god-knows-what-else with them? Or that Geniek just up and took sixty pieces of bread from those half-starving people, claiming that they had shirked their work responsibilities? Do you get me? He, a *Haeftling*, herding other *Haeftlings* to work! I see this and I am still unable to spit in the face of that 'old guard' from Auschwitz, Birkenau, Buchenwald, Lublin, Dachau . . .

JAN: Lager organization has gotten into their blood.

FRYDERYK: You're wrong. This isn't about organization; it's about the deliberate breaking down of human beings at every step with full awareness. It is a diving into the muck with complete relish, complete pleasure, a bestializing by those who themselves have already been transformed into beasts. It's jealousy, spitting on those better than you. It's pleasure at the sight of man turned monkey, with an angry, furrowed face and grasping paws. Do you know that in here they consider me a non-kosher clown, who has to kow-tow and re-tell farces and risqué anecdotes under the threat of losing the favor of his lordship who knows that this stinking room is a palace compared to the hell of life in the barracks?
(with increasing emotion)
They grab me so hard by the nose that I get tears in my eyes.

JAN *(with a shade of impatience)*: Fryderyk, you shouldn't give in to them.

FRYDERYK *(almost frantic)*: Do you know what ashes are? Blue scraps full of apparent life, turning dark and then white again? That's me. I'm an ash. These few months in the Lager have burned me up, completely wasted me. Only the past stirs within me still, like a blackened beam from a burned-out house, along which sparks flicker now here, now there, quick and shining with the potential for life and flame.

JAN: Oh, I suspect we'll be seeing you on the stage again.

FRYDERYK: Oh yes. With a broken back. Do you know what it's like to have someone put their finger under your ribs and shove it around while stupidly singing, "Tiu, tiu, tiu, my gentle graybeard, I need to tickle you"? Or rumple my hair, all in the guise of good humor, that hair which not so long ago was tragic Lear's gray crown!?

JAN: Fryderyk, you shouldn't get so worked up!

FRYDERYK *(maniacally)*: Or when suddenly during a game of cards one of the young punks calls you a 'jerk-off with professional status' . . .
(his voice shakes, his hands fly about)
you . . . who were Hamlet with a soul as blue as steel . . . who created a new era playing Ibsen and Strindberg. These rats bite you and undercut the value of your life, which you served selflessly. They gnaw at your heart till you become a clump of festering worms. Rabid rats . . . reared on corpses, the specimens of war. . . . Insanity.
Fryderyk clutches his head. Jędrzej awakens.

JĘDRZEJ: Oh good. Has uncle gone completely bonkers, or is he imitating that old circus sword-swallowing act? I mean, it certainly can't be indigestion that's bothering him.

FRYDERYK *(looks at him darkly, slowly regaining his composure)*:
Shut up, you ridiculous necrophiliac pup, and wait for the time when you'll be able to steal some gold teeth out of your friend's pocket.

JĘDRZEJ: Ah, yes. Uncle got mortadella for the day before yesterday's teeth and today he renounces it. Go figure.
Jędrzej smiles maliciously, shaking his head.

FRYDERYK: What I ate was not acquired for your false teeth but for the money you stole out of my jacket a couple of nights ago, remember?

JĘDRZEJ: Stole; didn't steal, my distinguished sir. And just where did uncle get the money in the first place if not from us, having won it at cards? And we organized it from the Hebes. Of

course, it wouldn't be proper for our gracious graybeard to take money directly from the *Haeftlings*, so he found a civilized way of wheedling it at bridge. *Nicht wahr?*
He turns on his other side and falls asleep. Geniek runs in and throws his hat on the nail. Grinning, Geniek goes to Fryderyk with an expression of sneering joy.

GENIEK: Hey, darling; what says our noble graybeard? I'm feeling very frisky, old hotsy-totsy, grand dame. Is a pig's ass pork?
He reaches with his finger near Fryderyk's stomach and midriff.

FRYDERYK *(forcing the joke)*: Not there. I need a massage nearer to my heart.

GENIEK: Massage, one might say, with pleasure, to the point of nausea, until one belches.
(tousles Fryderyk's hair)
Get on my bad side and I'll have your hair cut to make a *Streif*...

FRYDERYK: How come you're so cheerful, *Arlequino?*

GENIEK: Just imagine! I pumped the old man and there's going to be mash. We're going to make moonshine—oh, yes! Every day, my little dove. From morn 'til night, twenty-eight hours a day.
(shouts)
Hey! Kostek, rustle me some grub, or I'll fucking crack your skull!

KOSTEK (O.S.): What?

GENIEK: Cheese with sugar and meat and potatoes. Is the marmalade ready?

KOSTEK (O.S.): Not yet.

GENIEK: Well, best take care that I don't bury you, you miserable fuck.
Behind the wall those in the other room, recite in gloomy voices: "A dog pissed on my leg..." Kostek comes in with the food and places bowls and bottles on the table. Geniek sits down and starts eating.

GENIEK: I know, I'm a pig, but I am going to eat in front of you anyway, my children. After all, I am the *Lageraeltester*.
(He reaches behind him and takes a bottle of moonshine. Pours half a tumbler.)
Fryderyk, want a drink?

FRYDERYK *(lost in thought)*: Yes, I fell on my head.

GENIEK: If the noble old gentlemen finds moonshine unpleasant, he doesn't have to have any.
He eats greedily; the others watch him show off.
Delicate, little French poodle lost his mommy. In one ear and out the other.
(undoes the top button of his trousers)
Ugh, so much to take in.
(drinks from the bottle; gloomy silence all around)
We're going to have as much moonshine as our hearts desire, you sons of fucking country bitches. The *Lageraeltester* himself deigned to find sugar. Głowak, how many did you have to bury?

GLOWAK *(at the Schreibstube)*: Six.

GENIEK: And so, little shavetail, you regretted not being able to put some money in your pocket, eh? No matter. By tomorrow on the *Revier* four will grow cold, and you'll have unpaid work in your profession, my dear satanist, black shepherd, cobra crossed with a bat.

GŁOWAK: I'm not blind.

GENIEK: Watch your step, puppy, or I'll dump a bowlful of mustard on your head for being a wiseass.

GŁOWAK *(with a smile)*: A good joke is worth a bowl of mustard.

GENIEK: I'll be damned! Well, if you're a comedian, then I'm a fucking bishop. Say, did you place the crucifix on the graves?

GŁOWAK: Not yet. It's ready; it just has to be painted.

GENIEK: So go see whether it's still in the corridor or not.
Głowak exits, then returns a moment later very shaken.

GŁOWAK: What did you do with the cross? I ordered it to be made so that I could take it to the cemetery tomorrow. It isn't there.

GENIEK: The stupid asses probably used it for firewood. *Das ist auch Holz.*[3]

GŁOWAK: Impossible. Who?

GENIEK: Find out, little paraclete. Go, my young paralytic, spiritual drone, my gorgeous little Gypsy undertaker. A pig's ass is still pork.

FRYDERYK: I sense Jędrzej's hand in this.

GŁOWAK *(angered, loudly)*: Jędrzej!

JĘDRZEJ *(awakes; calmly)*: Misguided cherub, let me sleep, or I'll kick your priestly face in with my boot.

GŁOWAK: Did you chop up the cross?

JĘDRZEJ: Have you ever seen *Lagerkapo* Jędrzej chop anything?

GENIEK: So, *Kapucyn*?

GŁOWAK: Then who chopped up the cross?

JĘDRZEJ: Strange . . . I don't know; I kind of suggested it to Janek.

GŁOWAK: But why?

JĘDRZEJ: The potato pancakes, piggly-wiggly, couldn't be fried without the holy wood.

GŁOWAK: You didn't have any other wood?

---

[3] "It, too, is wood."

JĘDRZEJ: Dry? No.

GŁOWAK: So, Ivan made that crucifix for the graves, and you destroyed it.

GENIEK: All of a piece, you could say. Ivan, a communist, unbeliever, brandishes crosses; Jędrzej, on the other hand, an exemplary Catholic from birth, destroys them. A charming conundrum for communist Russia and his lordship the Pope.

JĘDRZEJ: It's of no consequence, but Ivan came to me about extracting teeth.

GŁOWAK: They hurt him?

JĘDRZEJ *(gentle irony)*: Absolutely.

GŁOWAK: He should go to the dentist on Wednesday.

JĘDRZEJ: It isn't a question of *his* teeth.

GŁOWAK: But you said they hurt him.

JĘDRZEJ: Of course, they hurt, numbnuts, because they're sitting in someone else's mouth. Namely a Jewish one, and the Jew isn't going to die until tomorrow and has to be watched. "D'you have pliers?" he asks me. "The Yid has a whole bridge made of gold."

GENIEK: Let him make another cross and swing it at the Jew's jaw. You could call it a Christian solution. The peaceful soul will wander off to paradise, having first spat out his teeth, which I claim for myself.
(Vorarbeiter Kominek enters with a Kommando list, which he gives to Głowak.)

KOMINEK *(to Głowak)*: The list is shorter. One escaped.

GENIEK: Who?

KOMINEK: Some little mangy guy, from the last *Zugang*. Number 12,243.

JĘDRZEJ: Let's congratulate *Herr Vorarbeiter* and wish him an easy death tomorrow. I wonder what punishment Fatso will choose: rope or bullet? Or, maybe he'll choke you with his own hands. He's a resourceful guy, with great theatrical instincts.

GENIEK: You know that Fatso pulled me aside today and told me that if someone escapes from a Kommando, five of that Kommando will be killed?

KOMINEK: That's news.

GENIEK: The latest. No skin off my teeth, though, because the sonofabitch didn't escape from the Lager; but you, Kominek . . . ?

JĘDRZEJ *(weighs his words)*: Ah well. He'll quietly hang, and Fatso's dog will be nipping at him as he does. I just ask, Kominek, that you don't bend your legs. All the hanged bend their legs, and then it's hard to fit them into the coffin.

GENIEK: The *Lagerfuehrer* knows?

KOMINEK: They telephoned him right away from the Kommando.

GENIEK: Then you're fucked. Get ready to die. Between five and you, Fatso will most certainly choose you because you should have been watching. At least you're certain of absolution; Głowak is handy. He's a very nice guy and for a chunk of bread he'll absolve you.

JĘDRZEJ: *Herr Vorarbeiter's* last wishes? We're listening . . .

GENIEK: And to think that Jędrzej burned the cross for pancakes. No matter. Głowak will accompany you anyway. He does it with a passion. He'd even kill his mother and father just to have clients for the cemetery. That's his apostolic nature. Perhaps you'll have a vodka? We'll even clink glasses with you, tomorrow's corpse.

KOMINEK: Give it. Moonshine?

GENIEK: Twenty-year old *Izdebnik.*
He pours a mug of liquid and offers it to Kominek, who gulps it down. Geniek drinks with him. The others look on.

GENIEK: How is it?

KOMINEK: Ugh. What is this? Tastes like soap.

JĘDRZEJ: That's a preview of tomorrow, when a soapy rope will tickle your throat.

GENIEK: I don't think so. A soapy rope for a *Haeftling*? That would make it worth dying. How many did you hang in Auschwitz, Kominek?

KOMINEK: I didn't hang. I worked by the crematorium.

JĘDRZEJ: See what piss-poor luck you have? You burned, and now you will be placed in unsanctified earth, patted down with a spade. Głowak will bark out a few curses in the Abyssinian language. I'd like to die like that myself.

GENIEK *(to Kominek)*: Get your ass out of here. I'm going to talk with Fatso again today. Maybe I can work something out. He's big on popularity.

JĘDRZEJ: I'll tell you what: Kiss Fatso's dog on the tail. Oh! He doesn't have a tail. Damn, that was your last hope. You'll hang; but don't worry, at least you won't drown.
Vorarbeiter Kominek exits.

FRYDERYK: You talked with Busch today?

GENIEK: Yes. That fat fuck is capable of anything. Just think: *Obersturmbahnfuehrer* of the Gestapo. You don't earn that rank for doing just any old thing. The prick's an hysteric and a sadist and nothing but evil looks out of his eyes.

FRYDERYK: There will be a hard *Appell* again.

GENIEK: Big fucking deal. Quit bitching, you gray-headed baboon. Damn! You're as pleasant as a case of the clap. Have some moonshine, will you?
(Geniek pours for himself.)

FRYDERYK: On Busch's grave.

GENIEK: He'll outlast you. Him and his dog. You don't have heart.

FRYDERYK: Heart?

GENIEK: You weren't in Auschwitz. You don't know what it means to have heart.
Offstage singing starts in the Lagerleitung quarters. A guitar can be heard; the squawk and rumbling of an accordion. They sing the famous tango, "The Night is Ours." Good, strong, male voices, trained and in unison.

FRYDERYK *(listening)*: Yes. Heart. I once had it.

GENIEK: Only the old guard knows what it is to have heart.
(drinks)
Christ! I've become a fucking whore.
(throws the mug at the door)
You see what it is to have heart? Another mug.
Głowak hands him a mug.

GENIEK: Głowak, you simpleminded shaveling, drink with me.

GŁOWAK: I don't drink.

GENIEK: Up your ass, then, pale Jesuit. Want something to eat?

GŁOWAK: That I can do.
Geniek throws him a quarter of the bread remaining on the table.

GENIEK: Here!

GŁOWAK: But without absolution.

GENIEK: Stupid ass, why would I ask you for absolution?
(smashes the mug on the table)
Fryderyk, will you have a drink, my friend? With an old Kamarado who saved your life and who will stand by you in every need?
(belches loudly)

FRYDERYK: Why are you hanging on me like a leech?

GENIEK: You have no heart. You weren't in Auschwitz.
He grabs a clay bowl and hurls it to the ground; then a second; then a third; saucers, jars, spoons, knives, any and all objects near at hand. Finally, he grabs a large bottle of moonshine, weighs it, but after a while carefully puts it down on the table.

FRYDERYK: And so, you don't have heart either?

GENIEK: Actually, I do, fuckface, and that's why I'm saving it. Fortune's fool, Lager poet, helper of the weary . . .
He seizes a clay figurine and throws it at the window; the panes come crashing inside beneath cloth. The figurine falls onto the Schreibstube and breaks.

GENIEK: Give me something else, or I'll rip your legs off, fucking piece of shit millionaires.

FRYDERYK: Perhaps now you'll throw yourself out of the window?
Jędrzej slowly gets off the bunk, crosses to the cupboard, takes out a few bowls, and hands them to Geniek who throws them against the door.

JĘDRZEJ: Please. Please. We will serve the *Lageraeltester*. All of us . . . Something else perhaps?

GENIEK: Give. Or I'll kill you.

JĘDRZEJ: There aren't any more. Perhaps *Herr Lageraeltester* will suggest going into the Block and finding the *Haeftlingen's* bowls? It will be done immediately. On the double! The *Lagerleitung's* room is near by. The boys will be happy.

GENIEK *(semistuporous, belching)*: Bring it.
He drinks. Jędrzej goes out and brings back a few bowls and mugs, all of which Geniek takes, throws, and breaks.

JĘDRZEJ *(smiling, eyes averted)*: Yes, yes, we're having fun now. Amusing ourselves, you could say . . . Very interesting.
In plain sight, he snatches up Geniek's box of tobacco and calmly begins to roll a cigarette. He pours some of the tobacco into the pocket of his jacket.

FRYDERYK *(to Geniek)*: Bravo! You've broken the dishes and there aren't any extra bowls. What are we going to eat off now?
(beat; sourly)
Of course! You'll take them away from the prisoners on the Block. There's only one bowl for four of them as it is.

GENIEK: Shut the fuck up, you half-assed, spineless piece of shit! What do you know? You have no heart, no struggle.
Distant sirens, then closer ones, and finally the camp air alarm signals. Nobody takes any notice of these, nor of the sounds of airplanes flying over the Lager. Offstage the same group sings a song about the sailors on the Albatross. Distant echoes of bombs can be heard, a purr and groan resounding from the hills.

GENIEK: We, the old guard, the old numbers . . . Do you know what number I have from Auschwitz?
(shows his tattoo)
See. 7000. 1940. We, the *Alte Garde*, we've survived everything and we'll survive this, too, because we are the future of Poland, the backbone on which everything will depend. You weren't in Auschwitz; you didn't see what we saw. For us, dying was like shitting is to everyone else. You don't know a goddamned thing, that's the problem. Did an SS man choke you half to death like Palitsch did me? Did you squeeze into a bunker, crammed with twelve others—in 9 square feet of space!—when the little high

window got frozen over from our breathing and you couldn't reach
it to wipe it clear? I was taken out for interrogation and the others
croaked, suffocated over the next few days, the window frozen
over. They were carried out before my eyes. Six days without eating
and to die from a lack of air! Have you experienced anything like
that? So what can you know? Did you see how the Russkies gave
a beating? How they'd pick a guy up and slam him to the ground
so that they'd rupture his kidneys. And he'd swell up and lie dying
for weeks on end. Or how they'd hold a victim under water in such
a way that he wouldn't drown. By the hour, in the Block gutters
where fucking *Holzschuhe* are washed. I saw a Kapo from Cologne,
a German Gypsy, built like that—
(demonstrates the wide breadth of the man's shoulders)
who was beaten in Buchenwald for half a day and then was carried
out in a wheelbarrow, a pile of meat vomiting blood, and dumped
behind the small Lager. And then I saw that pile of meat leap up
and run, blindly, with dislocated shoulders, to the gate, seeking
safety with the SS.
(He drinks.)
So what do you know, you old rat fuck? Huh? What the fuck do
you know? You didn't get to experience the Lager thanks to my
good graces. Did you see the first mass extermination at Auschwitz?
Were you there? In the evening, six hundred people were called out
and herded into Block Eleven. Nobody believed—nobody wanted
to believe—they would be shot. But already, in the morning wagons
were pulled through the Lager loaded to the top with corpses still
leaking blood like pigs. I myself pulled a wagon . . . and behind us
we left a broad trail, like a bubbling red stream. The wind blew
back the canvas and we saw the naked bodies, riddled with bullets,
with bared teeth and eyes wide open. For weeks I loaded corpses,
was a *Leichentraeger*. Two of us would pick up a body by its
extremities and swing it—hup, hup, hup—into the air and onto the
wagon where it would land among its shit-caked and foul-smelling
kinsmen. My first three days on the job, I couldn't eat a thing.
And I was hungry, friend. I'd've settled for anything: a crust of
stale bread or some soup made from rutabaga and old gramophone
records. But I couldn't eat. My hands were thick with fat from the
corpses and there was nowhere I could wash them.

(pause)
That's what times were like. And now you want me to regret the loss of a bowl? I've got bowls up the ass in the Block. Let those cocksuckers organize for what they need wherever they can, the way I organized old food cans from the garbage so that I could find enough peelings to make a half a cup of soup. Fucking money-grubbing, ass-fucking millionaires! What do I give a shit about them? Did you see my number? The first transport to Auschwitz, two years of penal Kommando in Birkenau, where organizing the dregs from SS lunches was hog heaven. I shit blood for two weeks after getting typhus—do you hear me? Typhus!—Wasn't able to eat a thing. People like me will be the future of Poland. We know what we have to do. Our Lager education will come in handy.
He spreads his hands on the table, puts his feet on the crossbars. He is sweaty; his hair is disheveled.
Offstage the voices begin to sing the Dubinshka, a song popular in the Lager.

GENIEK *(archly)*: You never saw the cannibalism in the Russian POW camp. The corpses that 'vanished' who knows where, who knows how. You couldn't cook, so the 'tovarisch' dispatched their buddies raw. Ate them. Like pickles!! And the Gypsy Lager? I was a *Pfleger* there. You can't imagine the shit that went on! Fathers sold their children. Girls from the age of twelve: sold. I myself bought one for a bottle of cognac and two loaves of bread. She was expensive because her virginity was guaranteed. And, my god, how the Jewish girls from the Folies Bergeres ran around! Everybody wanted them. In three days, they were finished . . .
Geniek falls into a gloomy silence, elbows on the table, gazing into the distance, drunk and full of images of the past.

JĘDRZEJ *(cackles; then speaks in a thin voice)*: I organized a fur once, from Canada, from some Dutch millionairess—roll mops or astrakhan, I can't remember what the fucking thing was called. I wanted to give it to my Julienne. And one of those conniving bastards grabs me by the ass and kicks me in the back. Stomps me down. I lost the fur and couldn't sit down for three days. The prick. And then his compatriots went and fucked Julienne and laughed in

my face. *Das spielt keine Rolle wer*[4].... God! She was such a beauty, one fine piece of ass.
(He makes an illustrative gesture with his hands.)

GENIEK: Or when they brought phenol in. Jews and non-Jews came to the Revier for medical help. Regardless of whether it was summer or winter, all of them had to strip naked. Didn't matter what you'd come for. You could have inflammation of the eye, a boil on your face, a frostbitten finger, everyone stripped naked and then stood for hours outside or in the cold, draughty *Revier* corridor. Then the poor suckers were pulled out and sent to the doctor. But the doctor didn't examine them, just gave them an injection straight to the heart. And the patient took four, five steps, left the room by a different door and fell into the *Pflegers'* open arms. Dead. That was phenol. You had to wait a long time for a slow, miserable death, so nature had to be helped a little. Sometimes scores of corpses a day went to the crematorium. And although word spread across the whole camp about this special medical procedure, the sick came regardless, and often precisely because of it. An easy death.

JAN: In Lublin I lay in the *Revier* for a month during the worst period of the sick being sent to the gas. Typhus. A *Pfleger* I knew laid me on some old rags in the attic. And forgot about me. Thousands of lice crawled all over me. There was nothing to eat. It was only when I got a parcel from home and offered him some that he brought me food. And he washed me, because I shat myself like an infant.

GENIEK *(to Fryderyk)*: See? See, you old pie-in-the-sky, gray-haired theatrical snob? There you have it. You live through all of that without changing one iota and I'll believe you've got the right idea. But first, try . . . *los, los . . . Caracho-Weg . . .* a whole day pushing a wheelbarrow at the run or humping a sack of cement on your back. "Move! Move! Move!!" And then at night endure *Appell* on top of it. Do you know what the *Appell* was like in Birkenau? Hours in the bone-chilling cold, with an empty pit instead of a stomach

---

[4] "It doesn't matter who . . ."

and the prospect of death if the escapee wasn't found. Twelve hours without a break . . . and every other minute . . . thud! . . . thud! . . . th ose who couldn't endure it would freeze to death lying in the snow. But before they could die, their loving friends would rob them of their wooden clogs or whatever rags they were wearing. Yes sir! And I know you never saw the march of muzulmen from the *Revier* to the *Waschraum*. A hundred yards. All the sick stripped bare in the hellish frost. And then, march! Go wash! Naked in the frost, people who couldn't move. No matter who. No matter how diseased. *Ganz egal; alle raus*! Did you ever see that march of emaciated naked people, tuberculoid, riddled with typhus, phlegmon, and diarrhea, stumbling in twos and threes, holding one another up despite the cold and the wind? Slowly. Slowly. . . . Sometimes it seemed the wind would blow them down like the leaves of some long past summer. Then into a scalding hot bath and back out again into the frost. A hundred yards. In a single day, a third of the sick went to the devil. But here, too, there was a method in the madness!
(Geniek drinks deeply, sloppily.)
So what can you tell me, huh?
Jędrzej takes Geniek's tobacco and paper off the table and rolls another cigarette.

JĘDRZEJ: My, my, my, that was some life! For a bottle of liquor from Canada, a thousand dollars. For a kilo of butter, ten gold watches. And all of it brought in by Dutch, Belgian, French, Polish, Czech—anywhere you damned well please—Jews. They came to work. Asked where their homes were. They brought seeds!! And an hour after their arrival, they were dead. Often they carried five, six suitcases. Some needed special wagons to carry all their baggage. The wife, children, dressed to the nines. They didn't want to believe it when they were told they were going to the gas. Next day, I passed the mail Block and couldn't believe my eyes. There was this long table mounded with loot. Good stuff: eyeglass frames, false teeth, gold watches, rings, religious articles, necklaces, medallions, cigarette cases, bracelets, pearls, diamonds—anything you can imagine. Dollars, pounds sterling, stocks—whatever anyone wanted. The SS men sorted through it, there was no one controlling them. And then everything was sent to Berlin. You kept whatever you could steal. We pigged out and drank ourselves silly, Canada you could say.

Jędrzej shakes his head. He climbs onto the bunk and lies down.

GENIEK *(to Fryderyk)*: Do you know what it means to have a position of responsibility in the Lager, Mr. Analyst Who Never Does Anything? It's the same as having no position. You have nothing. You die from hunger, from overwork. If you have responsibility, you croak because you must organize and they wear you down through intrigue—they prey on your stupidity or your wisdom. You can never figure out what will do you in. My best friend in the Gypsy Lager went up the chimney just like the others. You know why? His lover ratted him out. She was quite the dish; I was hoping to inherit her from him. But you know why she ratted him out? Because she was afraid she'd lose him. Simple, green-eyed jealousy. And the guy never even dreamed of cheating on her. Never. And what's most interesting: soon after they killed him, they killed her too. Bang, bang! Because she let it slip that they both secretly listened to the radio. And Kubik, that sonofabitch from Silesia, was killed by the people on his *Aussenkommando* because he was loyal to the Germans and did what he was ordered. He beat people to death with a stick, in cold blood. Ten, twelve, a day. As many as necessary. And how many kicked the bucket for the escapes of others? Do you think that, if I let people out of the Lager, my life would be worth as much as a thimbleful of fish piss? I'd have the SS on one hand and the noose on the other. I count on nobody, not even you freeloaders, you exalted lords of the Lager. Any one of you would cut my nuts off if you got the chance. You motherfuckers are all biding your time, waiting for an opportunity; but I'm no johnny-come-lately. You can't con me.

FRYDERYK *(shrugs)*: This is idiocy. The product of an overactive imagination. Nobody here is after your vaunted position, to which is attached a hunk of rotten meat stolen from the *Haeftling's* kitchen and the dubious honor of mediating between the Lager and the Germans.

GENIEK: You just let me find out that one of you has civilian clothing without a window or stripes! Or that a number's missing or a triangle. I promise you I'll put the screws to all of you.

FRYDERYK: There's no point threatening us; we all know that you're a prick only to a point. Besides, not one of us is going to make life harder for any of the others. There are plenty of other opportunities. And we all have family we don't wish to jeopardize . . .

JAN: Anyway, for us, plotting an escape assumes an unnecessary risk. You know that yourself. You can trust us; we have as much common sense as you do.

GENIEK: You don't drink; I don't know you.
Jan shrugs.

GENIEK: You can't throw a knife.

JAN: Nor betray.

GENIEK: And you don't beat people. So what kind of Kapo are you?

JAN: It's all the same to me. I don't need to be one.

GENIEK: What the fuck? Did I ask you?
Jan shrugs.

JĘDRZEJ: Don't be mad, popsy-wopsy; just don't be mad. You say yourself that you have beautiful greeny-blonde hair; it'll only turn gray.
He gently strokes Geniek on the shoulder with one hand, while, at the same time, snatching up the bottle of moonshine with the other; he drinks.

GENIEK *(without looking at Jędrzej)*: Put the bottle down, boy. Put that bottle down, merry prankster, or you'll get a double injection of chloride.
Jędrzej slowly lowers the bottle from his mouth.

JĘDRZEJ: Your mother must have married a fucking estate foreman because you've got eyes in the back of your head.

GENIEK: When necessary, the *Lageraeltester* even has eyes in his ass.
He reaches back, takes the bottle out of Jędrzej's hand, and takes a drink.
Lagerschutz 1 brings in three parcels of food, two with the characteristic Red Cross label and one with private markings which evokes general interest. He places the parcels on the table and leaves.

GENIEK *(reading the addresses on the parcels)*: Ah, Van der Bosch again.
(examines the contents of the parcel)
Nice. Ovaltine, American cigarettes, chocolate, bacon, powdered eggs . . .
(examines the second parcel)
. . . the same for Netter. Well, well . . .
(unpacking the private parcel; reads the address)
And this one for the kind-hearted Górecki, our lanky romantic. What did he get? Breads, yes, and butter . . . bacon . . . candy . . . a lemon. Sonofabitch, would you look at this?!
(pulls out a tiny bouquet of dried flowers tied with a faded ribbon)
Flowers! To a concentration camp no less, where bodies are crushed and people die from hunger. You'd have to be out of your fucking mind!
Whistling in derision, Geniek gestures as if the ridiculousness of the flowers has sent him into a swoon.

FRYDERYK *(thrilled, about the bouquet)*: How beautiful! Completely faded, like the vision of a rainbow.

GENIEK *(with contempt)*: A vision? More like useless junk. Probably grew in a shit pile behind a barn.

FRYDERYK: What do you know? They're beautiful . . . and they're necessary.

GENIEK *(visibly upset)*: Sure. You'll make three day's worth of soup out of them, give you the strength to jerk yourself off.

FRYDERYK: You're such an ass. Other than the hay, you don't see the world.

(picks up the bouquet)
See how they smell of freedom?

GENIEK: Of *what?*

FRYDERYK *(looking at the flowers)*: Freedom. And the human heart
and pure blue eyes filled with tears, yearning for someone who is
far, far away and will not, perhaps, ever return. In these flowers lives
the legend of our wasted lives, the beauty of the death camp. If our
lives are worth anything, it's only so far as to inspire resistance and
longing. You surely don't think your moonshine is worth anything,
do you? Or that your skill at smashing faces in accordance with
the new world order is of some real importance? Does the hunk
of gristle you gobble up each day have value? Does leading the
pathetic SS by the nose have value? These flowers not only represent
gentleness and a house at peace . . . a blue and quiet dawn . . . and a
bird's song . . . the touching of the heart; they are something more.
They suggest a different world, a good world which is fighting for
its life against the principles you have so eagerly adopted—although
occasionally still you drunkenly protest against them. No, the power
of these flowers is such that at this moment the camp does not
exist, the nightmare of life here has no purchase. There is only a
woman's hand offering a vow of faithfulness and love—

GENIEK: And on and on, good Jesus Christ, ad great nauseam.
The only thing your chickie, your faithful pussy, can offer you
from a distance is an excuse to jack off. My humble apologies, Mr.
Author-of-Childish-Delights, but I am not an idealist or a romantic.
Moonshine is my reality. A bone with a little meat on it is reality.
But these weeds?
He goes to throw the flowers into the corner of the room.

FRYDERYK *(stopping Geniek)*: Those aren't yours, moonshine realist.
You must give them to Górecki.

GENIEK: What? This grass?

FRYDERYK: Not grass. A symbol of what we suffer for in the
camp, the principles of life for which we give our last breath.

GENIEK *(who fully understands)*: A symbol . . .

FRYDERYK *(fixated on the flowers)*: Like a woman's hand at the moment of damnation, they stop time and create the illusion of happiness, a happiness which is beyond all bounds. They bring with them the charm of green fields across which the sun moves like a golden and radiant landlord. They arose from our earth, grew along the path over which her contemplative foot wandered.

GENIEK: "Contemplative foot"? Have you gone completely bat shit? What about that butter there? It comes from a cow's udder. Does it too constitute a celebration of Polish fields? After all, it arrived totally fresh.

FRYDERYK: Butter has practical value, so it can't be beautiful. But this bouquet is as splendid as a poem from a faded album, like a delicate touch on a keyboard, like youth, which always knows the impulses of the human heart. These flowers are Poland, which is both poem . . . and music . . . and youthful spirit.

GENIEK *(sneering)*: And butter can't be?

FRYDERYK: The Pakulski brothers are also a piece of Poland. But they don't adorn it the way these flowers do.

GENIEK: Very worthy merchants, those brothers. I always shopped at their place; but, as far as I know, they didn't trade in flowers.

FRYDERYK: You're just jealous that the bouquet wasn't sent to you.

GENIEK: Me? Jealous of that garbage?

FRYDERYK: Take care not to offend the gods!

GENIEK: Bunch of straw.

FRYDERYK: All right, then. Call Górecki. Let *him* tell us what these flowers mean to him.

GENIEK: Done. *Lagerschutze!*
Lagerschutz 1 enters.

GENIEK: Bring Górecki, Van der Bosch, and Netter.
Lagerschutz 1 exits.

GENIEK: We'll see what Górecki says when I make him choose between the parcel or the flowers.

FRYDERYK: Yes. We will see, broken barrel of moonshine. You think everybody is only a belly like you.

GENIEK *(thumps his fist on the table)*: Hey. Fuck you. Don't get cocky. You haven't won yet.
He hides the flowers in a drawer. Van der Bosch, Netter, and Górecki enter and stand by the door.

GENIEK: Van der Bosch!

VAN DER BOSCH *(French accent)*: Present.
Geniek throws him a parcel.

GENIEK: *Au revoir.*

VAN DER BOSCH: *Merci.*
Van der Bosch exits.

GENIEK: Netter.

NETTER: Yes.
Geniek throws him a parcel, which Netter catches.

GENIEK: Now beat it, "Judas Maccabeus" Netter.
Netter exits.

GENIEK *(staring at Górecki)*: Górecki. Listen. If someone sent you a bouquet of flowers, which would you prefer to have, the flowers or some grub?

GÓRECKI *(masking his unease)*: I'd take both.

GENIEK: Stop fucking around or I'll kick your silly ass all around the Block. And my leg's a mighty motherfucker. I want a straight answer here.
Geniek thinks for a moment. He seizes the bottle and takes a long drink from it.

GENIEK *(deliberately)*: If you had to choose between a package of fresh butter and bacon and jams and cakes, and a bunch of faded flowers sent to you from home, the stems tied with a ribbon— which would you pick? Think hard now. Remember you are in the Lager.

GÓRECKI *(without a moment's thought)*: The flowers.

GENIEK *(getting up off the chair)*: You'll be dead in three days, shit-for-brains, thinking like that. I know. Here's your package; and take care that your ass doesn't meet up with my foot. I've seen a lot of numbskulls in my day, but a fucking smack-off like you—expecting a garden party at the gallows—I haven't had the opportunity to see in a long time. Get out of here before I change my mind, you miserable sack of shit.
Geniek throws Górecki the package; Górecki exits silently. Jędrzej slowly gets off the bunk and backs out of the room.

FRYDERYK *(to Geniek)*: You didn't give him his flowers.

GENIEK *(angrily)*: What flowers? What is it with you and those fucking flowers?

FRYDERYK: You hid them in the drawer.
Geniek opens the drawer and takes the flowers out as though he didn't know that he'd hidden them there.

GENIEK: Ah, your perfect symbol of the human heart. Makes me want to puke.
(holding the flowers and staring at them)

So these weeds represent beauty and truth and Poland, is that it?
(through clenched teeth)
And a young woman sighing over that dumb ass I almost busted in half just now?
(silent for a moment)
And the value of life, meadows across which storks stride and frogs call—
(with a more forced irony)
on a sunny evening under a linden tree opposite the manor house?
(increasingly stressing the irony)
And blue, expectant eyes, and warm greetings, and muslin frills and colored ribbons?
(his sneering becomes false-sounding)
And ladylike sighs in the bedchamber and the moon's silver face watching motionlessly?
(painfully shaking his head)
Pink cherries and jasmines and a garden of white apple trees in bloom and that scent ... the scent of lilacs ...
(fighting with himself, his fingers crush the flower petals which fall to the table)
Son of a fucking bitch! I'm going to kill ... !
(goes silent, staring at the remains of the bouquet in his hand)
Flowers ... phantom bells ... little bells in the meadows—blue ... and dewy grass and golden marigolds which we picked in handfuls ... cornflowers full of a fresh scent ... childhood ...
(head sinking down to the table, he bursts into tears)
A time when ... I was still ... a human being.
Jędrzej enters. A smile on his face, his pockets stuffed, hands full of American cigarettes, obtained from those who received packages.

JĘDRZEJ: I told you, popsy-wopsy, to take a few drops of valerian ...
He deftly snatches up the bottle and drinks from it.

LAGERSCHUTZ & STUBEDIENST (O.S.): *Appell!*

Blackout (End of Act One)

Act II

The room as previously. It is after midnight. Geniek, partly covered with blankets, is sleeping on the lower bunk. Towels hanging by his head shield him from the lamplight. Fryderyk sits at the table; Jan next to him.

JAN *(completing a sentence)*: . . . but I don't know. Do you remember Thomas Mann's *Magic Mountain*? You come away from it with the sense that mountains not only don't cure, but create tuberculoids. And that was a repudiation of the prevailing wisdom in the sanatoriums, that the mountains promoted health. All I can say is, our camp is in the mountains and we have mainly tuberculoids and diseases of the lungs.

FRYDERYK: Did you know I lived for quite some time at Dr. Tourban's, whose sanatorium was the model for Mann's version? I call that chapter of my life "Dostoyevski's Revenge." A bit like *Die Fledermaus*. I went to the sanatorium to visit my friend, Count Palfi, a Hungarian officer and a formidable drunkard who had been diagnosed with tuberculosis and who'd been staying there for some months. You ate there under the *table d'hote* system, separate tables for small groups of people, and the guests at the tables were mutually acquainted. So I ate lunch one day with Palfi and Baron Schwarz, an ethnic Jew. Schwarz had just been made a Baron by Francis Jozef for some service in the realm of arms production since he was the owner of several large munitions factories. In those days, for whatever reason, it was fashionable among the Austrian aristocracy to use Jewish jargon. Now, on the previous day, there had arrived at the sanatorium members of the Todleben family, a very prominent Russian clan. In fact, the historic defense of Sevastopol during the Crimean War is credited to a Todleben, and these were close relatives of his, old and young women accompanied by the usual gaggle of nurses and servants. The noted Todleben had been a schoolmate of Dostoyevski who, in his later years, was sentenced to a penal colony in Siberia for his literary-revolutionary activities. There is a well-known letter from Dostoyevski to Todleben in which Dostoyevski, in very humiliating terms, asks for mercy for himself and his wife since both would not be able to survive the severe conditions in the penal colony. Todleben, who was famous by then, actually interceded for Dostoyevski, whose sentence was changed to deportation to some settlement. Tomsk, Omsk . . . I don't remember now. At that time, I barely knew Dostoyevski's work, but I respected him tremendously as a writer. As soon as the Todleben women appeared in the room, Schwarz glanced at one of them and, struck by her beauty, muttered to Palfi and me, "Who is that Venus of *mitzvah*?" I should add that in Hungary the Palfi family has a genealogy going back several hundred years; Schwarz's baronhood began with him. So when Schwarz asked in this fashion about one of the Todleben women, Palfi, with a magnificent gesture, turned to him and said, "My dear Schwarz, I have the right to talk Yiddish; you, as yet, do not." I joined in the conversation and explained that the Todleben family is known in Russia for saving Dostoyevski from death in Siberia. At this, from a nearby table, a young, plucky voice, a rich alto, suddenly responded, "The Todleben family is known above all for the defense of Sevastopol." I turned around. It was Miss Todleben speaking. "You will forgive me, madam," I said. "To me it is known above all for saving Dostoyevski. The other fact is of little importance." And I was about to add something I most surely would have regretted— that that beautiful nook by the sea had not yet come under the influence of Western culture, when Miss Todleben said, "For me, Dostoyevski's existence is of little importance." And that was how we met. Three months later, Natasha became my wife. We went to Davos and stayed in the Grand Hotel. She had a maid, beautiful little Jeanette, a Russian girl from the Baltic. Natasha and Jeanette, lugging the hand baggage, went upstairs, and I stayed for a while in the hall to find out about the bobsled races, which were to be held. I was walking by the kiosk when all of a sudden a book caught my eye, in a plain white cover on which was printed in red letters the word "Idiot." The author: Dostoyevski. Do you know it?

JAN: Yes. It's remarkable.

FRYDERYK: It had just been translated into German. I reached into my shirt for a few marks, paid for the book, then took it and settled down in a quiet corner of the hall and began reading. A quarter of an hour later, Jeanette came down, curtsied and said, "*Barynia prosit.*"[5] "*Siej czas przyjdu,*"[6] I replied and went on reading. I don't know how long I read, but, after a while the beautiful Jeanette stood in front of me again and, curtsying, said in a charming voice, "*Barysznia zowet barynia.*"[7] "*Skazi, milaja, czto siej czas, przyjdu,*"[8] I replied and went on reading. I finished—at six in the morning. I got up, caught my breath, and rushed upstairs to my wife's room. She was asleep, but the pillow was wet with tears. Such was the first night after our wedding, which Dostoyevski, whom Natasha had once so forcefully denounced, managed to ruin. Old times, good times. . . .

He lapses into thought, automatically rolling a cigarette.

JAN: Did you study in Munich, Fryderyk?

FRYDERYK: During its most beautiful years. When the *Jugendstil* was alive, when Kellermann, who lived in the same quarters as I did for a while, was starting out, when Wedekind was becoming vocal and well-known. There was a whole group of us artist types meeting at Lili Nevinny's, who was the daughter of a professor at the university and the Egeria of the literary crew and artistic rabble.

JAN: I know that atmosphere of aspiring young talent.

FRYDERYK: I remember a rather charming moment on my first evening there. It was in my twenty-first, or twenty-second spring. I can't recall who—perhaps Bernhardtt Kellermann—started talking about these two young people whose parents prevented them from sharing their passion for each another by locking them up in armor suits of glass, making it impossible for them to come close to each other. The youngsters then decided, "We'll rush at one another, and fall into each other's arms, even if we die when the glass shatters and cuts into our flesh." At that moment, Kellermann was called

---

[5] "The Baroness requests . . ."
[6] "I'll be along soon."
[7] "Baroness is calling for the Baron."
[8] "Tell her, dear, that I will come in a little while."

to the telephone, so he left without finishing the story, and Lili asked in her usual, slightly bored voice: "And which of you will dare to finish this tragic story?" pronouncing the word "tragic" with a sardonic sneer. "A very simple ending," I said. "The youngsters ran and fell into one another's arms without suffering the slightest injury, since the glass armor existed only in their imaginations and those of their parents." "A nicely conceived conclusion," Lili said, taking particular care with her words. "It allows us to see an entirely different reality." And that evening, when everyone was saying goodbye and it came to my turn, Lili held my arm, while saying farewell to the others. I stayed, and when we were alone she said to me, "So you think there were no other obstacles other than the imagination of the two young people?" And there weren't . . . ,

JAN (smiling): Ah. An historic literary moment.

FRYDERYK: Yes. What a funny and pleasant end to that adventure! You know, at the Simplicissimus bar there was a *Zahlmeister*, a headwaiter as we would say in Polish, who was a legendary figure as well. He was called Rudolf. Outwardly, he resembled the waiter in Zeromski's novella, *Pavoncelli*—the one called "Umberto," I believe. Rudolf counted with great drama, muttering in a deep bass voice over his torn notebook. And through his rasping whisper one could make out fragments of his calculations: "two coffees, 20; cake, 20: today is the 15th; together 1.20." And he was paid. It was sacred. "One schnitzel, 1.50; a bottle of wine, 1.20; bread, beer, cheese, 0.80 in total." Accompanied by a look from on high, through half-closed eyelids onto the ragamuffin waiting with trepidation for the verdict. Now, there was a custom at the Simplicissimus of bringing newly arrived Philistines to the bar to become acquainted with the habits of the Bohemians. Rudolf, who hated the Philistines, helped, of course. It normally ended with ordering chicken, duck, goose, wines and drinks for which the newcomer then had to pay since toward the end of the evening the rest of the company disappeared like smoke. One particular evening an elegant gentleman came into the Simplicissimus and introduced himself to us as Von Weinberg, a banker from Frankfurt am Main. Rudolf brought this Philistine to the table where several of us were sitting, promising he would enjoy a good time with us. We did what we could, and it was all the easier because Weinberg understood our jokes and enjoyed himself as much as we did. He paid the entire sum of money without blinking. The following day I received a letter and an invitation from him. In it, he asked me to add however many names of my colleagues as I wished to the invitation and to bring them to a ball he had arranged for his fellow bankers, whom he wished to entertain with our splendid jokes.

JAN: Nothing easier and nothing harder.

FRYDERYK: Precisely. We decided to respond and our letter subsequently became famous in all of Munich's artistic world. After consulting my friends, I wrote back that unfortunately we could not come to his ball because that same evening we were arranging a party with amateur performances in one of our ateliers. However, we invited him to come to our party and to bring with him several bankers—with a view to giving the artists some fun. Von Weinberg understood only too well, found himself in a tight spot, and came to me the following day with apologies, explaining that his writing of the letter had been awkward since he had no intention of getting at us. At the same time, he invited me to come visit him for the summer, to Frankfurt am Main. Now, I should add that this was the time of Oscar Wilde's triumphant *Salome,* which was being played as an opera to the music of Strauss. Late one evening at a masked ball, I saw Lili dressed in priestly Eastern rags, and I went up to her and sang the opening fragment of that opera: *"Wie schoen is Prinzessin Salome heute Abend."*[9] Which charmed her very much. Now, back to Von Weinberg. Two years later I went to visit him to go hunting and I met a very young, but talented painter whom I had helped a little when he was a student. I wanted to go with him that evening to one of the Frankfurt bars, but he turned me down because he was to be introduced to a beautiful young woman, who was both very attractive and very intelligent. "But, Fryderyk," he said, "if you truly wish to help me, tell me, you who are such a conqueror of female hearts, how to begin a winning conversation with such a woman." "Hm," I said, "I once managed to rouse some admiration by singing the opening verse of Wilde's *Salome.*" And I taught him the verse. We even rehearsed it on the piano. Finally,

---

[9] "How beautiful princess Salome is this evening."

relaxed and full of enterprise, the painter took off for the arranged meeting humming along the way so as not to forget: "*Wie schoen is Prinzessin Salome heute Abend.*" We planned to meet the next morning in the famous Frankfurt *orangerie* so that he could tell me how things had worked out. He came, but he seemed strangely gloomy and embarrassed. "Was it a success?" I asked. "Too much so," he replied. "The moment she heard that verse, she grabbed me by the arm and said, 'So, you know Fryderyk! Where is he? I must see him.' I told her that you would be waiting here for me today. She'll be here in an hour!" And that's what my last meeting with Lili Nervinny was like.

JAN: You're bringing me into literature through the kitchen door today, Fryderyk.

FRYDERYK: Yes. I'm hoping in the future to write my memoirs. After all, I was at the creation of Simplicissimus, which was brought into being by the prevailing atmosphere in the bar of the same name, whose owner was Keske Kobus, an ex-model of Stuck. I was part of that scene where Wedekind performed on the guitar, where one evening Chaliapin at the dawn of his fame sang Russian folk songs in a bass voice, where the divine Eleonora Duse and Sarah Bernhardt and the satirist Heine passed through, where Thoma and Rilke, still young and unknown, came by. I had the good fortune to see the beginnings of contemporary French art and music. Next to me, Picasso created the first of his works, Debussy played. I took part in creating theatre with Rheinhardt who was financed by my father among others. I had the fortune to spend time in Austria where the exiled Meyrink wrote his political satires. As a young diplomat, I managed to get to know the court of Nicholas II, Francis Jozef, and Wilhelm II; I witnessed the behind-the-scenes negotiations and trivialities. I studied in England at Oxford . . .

JAN *(deep in thought)*: A large chunk of time . . .

FRYDERYK: Yes. A very large chunk of time, well lived. And it all roils inside me here. In this lousy place. It weighs on me, if you know what I mean. To have achieved so much, lived through so much. Despair overwhelms me sometimes. There is much still to do. So much . . .

JAN: I expect to see you at work again, Fryderyk.

FRYDERYK: Don't delude yourself. It's too late.

JAN: No, it's not too late. I remember you from before the war.
It was at a jubilee or an academy in honor of some homegrown
national holy day.—The devil take every last one of them!—You,
among others, recited a poem. Wait! ... yes ... a woman's first and
last name in the title ... No. "Halinka and the Lord God." Barendt's.
That was a new era in declamatory art. Do you remember it?
Fryderyk nods his head.

JAN *(animated)*: Could you recite that poem? Now?

FRYDERYK: Of course. Nothing could be easier.

JAN: Please, then ...
Fryderyk sits on the table and recites.

FRYDERYK:
You say that you've lost your way.
A challenge of years and worries
Has weighed so heavily on your heart
And tested your love for Him
You no longer know how to meet Him
Or whether you even need Him.
Life.—Ah! Such an unsweet thing
And its color so funereal
That it is black and painful,
In tears, first and foremost—
And later—we look at ourselves
With such indifference
That we walk benumbed, not seeing
The days turning into years.
And as for Him?—No part of our hearts
Can find Him in us or above us.

Now, me?—I'm just an old doormat.
You know me and know I don't believe that stuff—

I advise you to go out at twilight
And walk along the bright blue fence
To the outskirts of town, nearly deserted,
Where the lamps shine hard with heavy tears.
Go up in the evening free of sorrow,
You who have marked yourself in tragedy.
Go, and you'll see Him opposite
The path to the eternal city,
His hat just a bit too big
With a golden brim of fire—
His shoes worn and old,
Caked with mud up to His ankles—
And pale, glassy eyes that burn
With an unquestionably godly light.
You'll see His coat, a coat which now
Surely is an otherworldly coat,
And stubborn wisps of hair,
Gray, and blowing in the wind,
And an odd goodness on his face
Which itself begs for goodness—
The wind will blow with a whip of rain
Like a wave lashing in from the side.

And it will happen here in Hanover
On a narrow, cobbled street
That God will take His arms
And gather the girl to His heart.
The homeless girl, the man homeless in eternity;
The lost child, the lost man in love—
You will burst out crying together
Under the radiance of the streetlight.
Then you'll go to the beer garden
Which boldly presents itself—
And you'll sit in an isolated booth
Over a stein of beer or some cider—
So much in love with each other
As only God is in man—
As only the Passerby is in you—
Perhaps with a tear on your lashes.

You'll say your last words—
Quietly, as quietly as possible—
And your hearts will spin
The late hour into a glistening net.

And God will, stroking the girl's
Golden hair with his tired
Hand, confess that
He did not defend you from yourself;
And you will believe all of His woes
And the loneliness of His days and their despair;
In the corner a gramophone—muted—
Will tender the undertones of a song.
And the Lord God with hands of kindness
Will gild your heart—
Half dead and cold with love—
So it will be the same but different.
And you will weep for joy
On that wintry and rainy evening
In the beer garden, your golden hair washing
Away the shadow of God's white feet.

JAN: Once during the war, when I was hiding out in a Polish manorhouse, I heard that poem recited . . .
(taking a deep breath)
It's over. Sometimes memory is as strong as the jaws of a wolf. It grabs and won't let go.

FRYDERYK *(his hand on Jan's shoulder; smiling)*: Especially the memory of those blue eyes . . .

JAN *(also smiles)*: Especially those blue eyes . . .

FRYDERYK: For you. But what about me?
(sighs)
My last years; my last words . . .

JAN *(gently)*: Come now, Fryderyk . . .

FRYDERYK: I would like to hear the sounds of the forest again, the murmur of beeches in March or April when the mountain wind blows, smelling of early, damp, and full-of-cold spring. When the sky is as azure as a ribbon, and the lakes reflect the over-flight of clouds. Once more to smell the ploughed fields, to walk a slushy path when the first white chamomile . . .

JAN *(in thought)*: . . . blues eyes looking at you once again . . .

FRYDERYK: You will see those blue eyes again!
A shout in the corridor. Quick footsteps off stage. Lagerschutze 1 and 2 rush in breathless and terrified.

LAGERSCHUTZ 1: *Lageraeltester!*

LAGERSCHUTZ 2: They've escaped!

FRYDERYK *(turns around quickly)*: Who? Where?

LAGERSCHUTZ 1: Two from Block 4!
Geniek moves the bed curtain. Sleepy and tousled, he sits up on the bunk.

GENIEK: Quiet! Or I'll smack the shit out of all of you. Who escaped?

LAGERSCHUTZ 1 *(under clear duress)*: We were escorting two men from the woods in the dark and came upon someone lying on the ground. All of a sudden, he jumped up and ran off into the darkness. We checked the bunks. Two people are missing from Block 4.

GENIEK *(severely)*: Which two?

LAGERSCHUTZ 1: Alex and Pawłowski.

GENIEK: And they haven't gone organizing, you're sure?

LAGERSCHUTZ 1: Impossible.

GENIEK *(stares at the Lagerschulz; then shouts)*: Głowak! Where is he? I'm going to kill the bastard!
Głowak runs into the room half-dressed.

GENIEK: Quick. Get Alex and Pawłowski's numbers from the *Schreibstube* together with their personal cards. Move! MOVE!!
Głowak runs to the files and begins searching.

GENIEK *(to the Lagerschutze)*: It's dark out?

LAGERSCHUTZ 1: Very.

GENIEK: And the guards know nothing?

LAGERSCHUTZ 2: So far, no.

GENIEK: Was there a lot of shouting during the chase?

LAGERSCHUTZ 1 *(naively)*: None.

GENIEK: You didn't shout?! Are you kidding me, Jas? Maybe you didn't run after them at all!

LAGERSCHUTZ 1 *(shrugs)*: It was dark. Where were we going to run?
Geniek buttons the top buttons of his trousers very quickly, puts on his striped prison jacket, smooths his hair with a quick gesture of the hand.

GENIEK: Głowak!—or I'll smack you from here to fucking China—where are those goddamned cards?

GŁOWAK: Wait! I have to find them first!
(He searches.)

GENIEK: *Schnell, du Arschloch, bloederhund. Speckjaeger.* I have to be the first one at the *Lagerfuehrer*'s, even before the guards.
(to the Lagerschutze)

Where are the wires cut?

LAGERSCHUTZ 1: We didn't look. They're electrified.

GENIEK: You searched the whole Block?

LAGERSCHUTZ 1: Yes.

GENIEK: We need to organize an *Antreten*. Line people up in fives, check the number.
(to the Lagerschutze, who are preparing to leave the room)
Not you.
(calls out)
Bloedeaeltester! Now! On the double!

CZESIEK (O.S.): Coming.
He enters.

GENIEK: Take one *Lagerschutze* from each of the two Blocks and organize an *Antreten* in Barracks 4. Get the Block elder there to help you check the number of people. The *Lagerschutze* on that Block are on my side. Wake up the *Lagerschutze* Kapo.

CZESIEK: Done.
He exits.

GENIEK *(shouts)*: Głowak! Or I'll bounce a bowl of mustard off your head! Is it impossible now to find anybody in those fucking files?

GŁOWAK: All right! All right! I've got them!
He hands Geniek two cards.

GENIEK: Follow me, *Lagerschutze*.
He takes a flashlight and leaves. The Lagerschutze follow him.

FRYDERYK *(after a moment)*: What a lot of hubbub about the carrying out of responsibilities! He couldn't let the boys get farther away before he gave chase?

JAN: This is a Lager, Fryderyk. How could he be slow to carry out his responsibilities, if the *Lagerschutze* informed him about the escape?

FRYDERYK: He could have searched through the files for half-an-hour, or checked the names or numbers of the escapees.

JAN: That wouldn't work. Any messing around, and he ends up six feet under.

GŁOWAK: I did what I could, but I only managed five minutes. What's worse is that Busch arrived today. That fat slob and his dog are bad news . . . .

FRYDERYK: Alex is very smart. He must have had civilian clothes ready.

JAN *(thoughtfully)*: The night is dark . . .

FRYDERYK: This will prove an interesting development for Busch. After announcing that for every escapee he'll shoot five prisoners, two people break out that same night. There should be ten corpses tomorrow.

JAN: That announcement concerned escapes from the Kommandos.

FRYDERYK: Only because he didn't anticipate escapes from the camp.

JAN: And that's why Geniek will persuade him not to commit a massacre. He knows Fatso's weaknesses—how much he needs to be well-liked.
Czesiek bursts in.

CZESIEK: Wh-wh-where is Geniek?

FRYDERYK: He went to the *Lagerfuehrer*. What's happened?

CZESIEK: I c-c-can't account for s-six people on the fourth Block. They're not there.

Jan whistles through his teeth.

FRYDERYK: Thirty corpses tomorrow.

CZESIEK: A-a-and that will be chiefly from among *us*, the *Lagerleitung!*

FRYDERYK: Not to worry. There are at most fifteen of us. Even Busch isn't capable of killing a person twice.

CZESIEK: G-got to run, search. T-tell Geniek when he comes, that it's s-six people short.
He exits.

FRYDERYK *(purring)*: Ah, this is starting to get serious. I'm not going to sleep all night because of Głowak's damned *Schreibstube*.

JAN: Let's wait for more news. After all, things can change in an instant around here.
Geniek runs in, both Lagerschutze behind him.

FRYDERYK: Did you go to the *Lagerfuehrer's?*

GENIEK *(nettled)*: Yes. I made the report.
(to the Lagerschutze)
Come here.
He stands the Lagerschutze under the lamp and studies them. One has a black eye and a bloody cheek; the other is caked with mud.

GENIEK *(to the Lagerschutze)*: You want to live?
Lagerschutze 1 and 2 nod their heads.

GENIEK: Then this is what you are to say: One of you—
(points to the bloodied Lagerschutz)
—was escorting the Russkie from the shed to the Block, and in the darkness you came upon a prisoner lying on the ground. He sprung up and hit you in the head with a stick, then ran off. You chased him, but he surprised you and punched you in the eye and then vanished into the darkness. Having been punched in the eye, you stopped and summoned the other *Lagerschutz* who, together

with you, searched the area around the Block. Afterward, you went to the Barracks and discovered two people missing from the bunks. Get it?
Lagerschutze 1 and 2 nod their heads.

GENIEK: And even if Fatso smashes your teeth in and threatens to shoot you dead, you stick to that story.
(to the Lagerschutz covered with mud)
Let me see.
(He examines him carefully.)
Good.

FRYDERYK: Geniek, Czesiek was here and said he was missing six people.

GENIEK: That's better. I'm going right to the *Lagerfuehrer! Raus!*
He exits with the Lagerschutze in tow.

FRYDERYK: Why this comedy? As if it weren't enough to simply report the escape of a few prisoners.

JAN: Wait, Fryderyk. We don't know what happened. And in any case, it's important that the SS are convinced that the *Lagerschutze* are in earnest. This isn't trivial stuff.

FRYDERYK: But this hustle-bustle is so ham-handed, so melodramatic.

JAN: Like everything in the Lager, it's done for the SS, not us.
Jędrzej enters, goes to the bunk, and hides a few items under the pillow. Then he opens a can of pineapple and begins to eat.

FRYDERYK: Already you've stolen? How did you manage that?

JĘDRZEJ: I was strolling through the Block and I pointed out to this asshole that he hadn't made his bed. He turns around to straighten the sheets and . . .

FRYDERYK: He didn't protest? Quarrel with you?

JĘDRZEJ: How could he? I'm the Kapo.
(offers the pineapple)
Want some?

FRYDERYK *(shaking his head)*: Were you on the fourth Block?

JĘDRZEJ: Yes. Everything's in order.

FRYDERYK: Meaning?

JĘDRZEJ: I have a can of condensed milk and sugar.

FRYDERYK: That you stole. I know. I'm asking about the escape.

JĘDRZEJ *(greedily licking out the rest of the pineapple)*: The cocksucker fell asleep behind the wires.

FRYDERYK: Who?

JĘDRZEJ: The guard. I approach with a flashlight and I shout: "*Posten! Posten!*" And I get nothing. Dead silence. So I flash the light around and there he is, snuggled in his coat, a hat over his ears, leaning against the stone sleeping. Now I yell: "*Posten*, come quick, the *Lageraeltester* has to be reported to the *Lagerfuehrer* because inmates have escaped." And he says to me, "I can't come off the watch. Wait until morning." "*Bis wan? Das ist unmoeglich!*"[10] I shout. "People will have gone far." And that idiot grins at me and says, "No problem! No problem! We've got electrified wire." Then the sonofabitch wraps himself back up in his coat. Finally, Geniek showed up and cursed him out.

FRYDERYK: And why did you bloody the *Lagerschutz*?

JĘDRZEJ: That was Heniek. He busted up Janek right after he met up with him in the doorway to the Block. Didn't even blink. He had a chunk of wood in his hand and bashed the fuck in the head with it. And then he went after his face. The boy's crazy like that.

---

[10] " 'til when? That's impossible!"

FRYDERYK: But why?

JĘDRZEJ: Uncle, what planet are you living on? The *Lagerschutz* was making it up.

FRYDERYK: Making what up?

JĘDRZEJ: The escapees had been gone for hours. The *Lagerschutze* didn't notice it until after the *Appell*. Those guys had to have skipped before nine o'clock when people were going to bed. And that's why you got the fairy tale song-and-dance.

FRYDERYK: I don't understand.

JĘDRZEJ: It's impossible for anyone in the short time between meeting the *Lagerschutze* and the beginning of the search to cut through several electrified wires and split. It had to have happened much earlier. And the best time for escapes is the first hour of dusk.

FRYDERYK: Did you check the wires?

JĘDRZEJ: What for?
(He licks the inside of the can.)

FRYDERYK: Do you think the Germans will be stupid enough to believe that story?

JĘDRZEJ: And you, Uncle?

FRYDERYK *(deep in thought)*: So it was a question of saving the *Lagerschutze* . . .

JĘDRZEJ *(smiles, shaking his head)*: Oh, Uncle's such a sweetie, he is. "Saving the *Lagerschutze*." Most amusing. Uncle is so naive, he probably still believes in the Immaculate Conception.

FRYDERYK *(ignoring Jędrzej's tone)*: So, what was it all about, then?

JĘDRZEJ: It's about us. Us! The rest is garbage. The *Lagerleitung* could hang for such a thing. After all, it's Geniek who chooses the *Lagerschutze.*

FRYDERYK: Let's hope, at least, that those people escape.

JĘDRZEJ: They'll escape. Alex is crafty old bird; and he's leading the way.

FRYDERYK: How do you know?

JĘDRZEJ: I sold him a jacket a week ago. He gave me some jam for it, which you, Uncle, if I remember correctly, enthusiastically praised.

FRYDERYK: A simple matter.
(beat)
After the war you won't need to bow to me, Jędrzej, when you meet me on the street.

JĘDRZEJ: After the war? And what am I going to be doing after the war? There will always be war and there will always be Lagers where people like me will come in handy.
He takes a flashlight out from under the bunk and exits.

JAN: This is not good news. But Fatso is playing for popularity.

FRYDERYK: He's a very unpleasant man.
There is silence. Then a distant scream, a dog's bark, and strange howling and yelping that could be animal or human. Followed by the murmur of voices. "Strom! Strom!" can be heard.

FRYDERYK: Do you think they've caught them?
He listens attentively.

JAN: I doubt it. What would they be doing for so long?
Jędrzej enters, approaches his bunk, takes a box of tobacco from under the mattress, then goes to the open door.

JĘDRZEJ: You, vice-count, my lord with the wind-jacket, come here!
Jew 2, bedraggled, enters and takes off his jacket.

JĘDRZEJ: Here. Two cigarettes worth and two papers.
He gives Jew 2 the tobacco and takes the jacket.

JEW 2: Mr. Kapo, can I change Kommandos?

JĘDRZEJ: What for?
He examines the windbreaker and tries it on.

JEW 2: They beat us there. And I have a wife and children I'd like to return to.

JĘDRZEJ: What the fuck are you talking about, needle-dick? What's a change of Kommando to you? You're going to croak before the war is over anyway. Get the fuck out of here!
He throws the Jew out of the room, then hides the jacket under the straw mattress.

JĘDRZEJ: They've got shit for brains. The Semites fucking want to go home! That's priceless!
(to Fryderyk and Jan)
Want to know what I did? But don't tell anyone.
Jan nods his head.

FRYDERYK: What?

JĘDRZEJ: Pourtales died on the *Revier*. I told them to take the corpse and shove it into Czesiek's bed. Czesiek is going to gag for days when I remind him how green Pourtales was and how his body was covered from head to toe in shit.

FRYDERYK: That's your style, all right.

JĘDRZEJ: Hey. No smart remarks, Uncle. They get on my nerves.

FRYDERYK: Up your ass.

JĘDRZEJ (*smiles and shakes his head*): You could say there's a double meaning in that. Terrific. Heh, heh, heh. Very interesting. Uncle is adapting to his surroundings, eh? Maybe you'd like a corpse in your bed?

FRYDERYK: Slow down, whippersnapper. Go get some sleep. You're looking a little funereal yourself.

JĘDRZEJ: Hey. Don't get personal. I've handled my share of shit; I'll survive. I'm *Alte Garde*. From a good family. Fuck me over twice if I don't dance at Uncle's funeral.

FRYDERYK: That won't be difficult.

JĘDRZEJ: Ah, Uncle's afraid. Uncle doesn't have Auschwitz training. If, like me, Uncle had sat every day on a pyramid of corpses that had been pulled out of the gas chamber and were awaiting the crematorium, and if Uncle had seen those hands, feet, heads, bellies, twisted red, black, green and brown with shit, women, children, men—and every day at that!—and had Uncle had to eat his breakfast with hands pulled out of that human shit, Uncle would have a different perspective. Independent thoughts—ho, ho ho—some imagination, you might say, spitting at wornout customs. The wisdom of Solomon would come up to Uncle and knock on his empty little head into which the wind blows platitudes about humanity with a heavy dose of Sunday school teachings. Yes, Yes . . . *Geniek runs in; behind him, Czesiek, two Lagerschutze and a few others.*

GENIEK: Głowak, quick, did you take out the cards of the remaining four escapees?

GŁOWAK: No. You didn't say anything.

GENIEK: Idiot! Do you have shit in your head instead of brains? You don't know that I have to give the personal data to the *Lagerfuehrer?*

GŁOWAK: Yes, I know, but I don't have the names of the escapees.

GENIEK: And would it be too great a task, O Eminence, to ask Czesiek?

CZESIEK: Here. Have it.
He hands Głowak the card with the names.

GENIEK: Hurry up, asshole, or I'll strangle you myself. The shit has hit the fan.

FRYDERYK: Did they catch somebody?

GENIEK: Worse.
(takes a bottle of moonshine from the cupboard and drinks)
I'm thirsty, goddammit, and tomorrow my liver will be shot to hell.

FRYDERYK: What happened?

GENIEK: Fatso's dog jumped onto the wire.

FRYDERYK: And killed itself?

GENIEK: No, he turned into a bouquet of flowers.

JAN: There are going to be corpses for certain.

FRYDERYK: That dog was his whole world once the war took his son.
(beat)
The wires were electrified. So, what we were hearing was the dog howling.

GENIEK: Fatso's huffing like a fucking steam engine. A volcano. Everybody's under threat of the revolver, whip, machine gun, artillery. If one of those six falls into his grasp, that fat fuck will beat him to death with his own hands. He's like a rabid weasel. And it's his own fucking fault. I mean, who in his right mind would let a dog that sniffs corpses off the leash? The fucking beast had been wading in dew. He jumped onto the wires full force, wanting to get to his master, and fried in an instant. For a moment there, I thought Fatso would try to save the dog and meet the devil himself; but he stopped short. So, have you got the cards?

GŁOWAK *(hands Geniek the cards)*: There.

GENIEK: I'm off. We'll see what that tub of guts is capable of.
(to the Lagerschutze)
You remember what to say?

LAGERSCHUTZE 1 AND 2: Yes.

GENIEK: The dance is about to begin . . .
(drinks the moonshine)
Yes, the dance is about to begin. Which of you wants a swig?
One after another a few men drink.

GENIEK: And now—Off we go, kicked in the ass through glasses! Ta-dum, ta-dum, the dance begins. And let one of you get into a tizzy and start talking stupid, I will squish you like a fucking cockroach. Let's go!
They exit.

JAN: This is monumental. And that dog is a pyrrhic victory. Somebody's going to pay tonight.
One shot, then another, is heard.

JĘDRZEJ: Guess I'd better go order a coffin.

FRYDERYK: Make that two.

JĘDRZEJ: One loads the bodies of the emaciated *Haeftlings* two to a coffin. And that, only while they're being transported. Afterward, the naked are thrown out into the pit and the planks of wood are returned to the Lager to await the next corpses. By now Uncle should know these things.
He exits.

FRYDERYK: How can one talk to such people in the words of Mickiewicz, or the sounds of Beethoven's *Pathetique*? It's all lukewarm water to their nerves and brains, which require disturbances in order to cause them to react.

JAN: For the old *Haeftling*, neither friends nor nation nor humanity exist. There's a Kamarado for making plans, there's a companion for moonshine, and there's an enemy if what's at stake is a threat to his well-being. Enough with humanity and kind-heartedness; enough with reason and self-examination. There's rivalry over a morsel of bread, over a bowl of soup; battle over the function of *Vorabeiter*; a spreading of intrigues. An old Haeftling is not an animal any more, but a half-crazed brute, unpredictable in his reflexes and actions. A National Socialist upbringing—the leather scourge, the stick, murder, gas, hunger, lying, refined cowardice, and doses of unimaginable defilement—and in the end we see the results. The better ones were turned to dust, the worse into . . . hyenas. One has to pay for one's life—and steeply at that—beyond what it's worth; and a payment of that kind precludes solidarity and honesty. And if one adds to that the need for never-ending self-intoxication, the need for slaughter, for robbery, turmoil, and conquest . . . A National Socialist upbringing, indeed. The product of pathological narcissists—adroit, long-armed monkeys.

FRYDERYK: Do you remember Sherriff's *Journey's End*? I played one of the major roles in it. A horrifying play, and yet how beautiful, how clean in comparison to what goes on here. You know, I can no longer find in myself faith in the right of a country to demand this kind of service from its citizens. A nation can demand life or death, but this kind of degradation? Sometimes the words 'honor,' 'God,' 'art,' and 'law' seem silly to me, so that I see no basis on which I can stand. There seems only one thing: a bottomless pit, without light, without hope from which I can't even manage to grasp resignation. Nation. Faith. What used-up, wornout tokens they are! Counterfeit coppers covered with rust, in the face of the evil which surrounds us.

JAN: Maybe we need to address these problems more simply: The more complicated they are, the more directly we attack them. There is indisputably something called humanity; and since humanity exists, its existence needs to be made easier, needs to be ennobled and refined. Nations have precisely this role, that of shaping a culture, always with the good of the whole in mind. From this point of view, a few of the simplest principles would be enough to combat evil for evil lies within the human heart and is that which harms a human being. Evil is murder, robbery, lying. Of course, change has to begin inside one's self . . .

FRYDERYK: Then, you reject the entire metaphysical superstructure.

JAN: Rather. I have plenty of work as it is.

FRYDERYK: And you agree to pass it by like this? What about notions of grandeur?

JAN *(shrugs)*: One more delusion; perhaps the most bewitching.
Czesiek enters the room lugging a terrified prisoner.

CZESIEK: S-stand here and wait for the *Lageraeltester*.
(turns to the others)
O-one of the six escapees. We found him in between the Barracks. A Uk-ukrainian son of a whore.

THE UKRAINIAN: *Shcho?*[11] I weren't running.

CZESIEK: We'll see; we'll see. G-Geniek hasn't been here yet?

FRYDERYK: No. How did you catch this one?

CZESIEK: He j-jumped out of the darkness like a scared rabbit. Probably to organize something. I don't think he was trying to escape, but he's as good as dead anyway. He's a suspect, and Fatso will seize the opportunity to avenge his d-dog.

UKRAINIAN: *Ja nie chatiel biezat. Ja byl tylko w uborkie.*[12]

---

[11] "What?"
[12] "I didn't want to run away. I was in the latrine."

CZESIEK: W-we'll see, *tovarisch moj*. You j-just stand here and wait for the *Lageraeltester*.
Czesiek exits.

FRYDERYK *(to the Ukrainian)*
How did they know what you were doing? They said you went out to do some organizing. Understand?

UKRAINIAN: *Da, panimaju. Ja byl w uborkie.*[13]

JAN: Leave it alone, Fryderyk. You won't be able to help him.
Geniek runs in.

GENIEK: Głowak, call those *Schneiders* to me.
He hands him a card with numbers. He notices the Ukrainian standing in the corner.
And what's this here?

FRYDERYK: Czesiek brought him in. He's suspected of trying to escape. One of the six.

GENIEK: Ah, that's different! We've won the game. *Ty gdie chadił?*[14]

UKRAINIAN: To the latrine.

GENIEK: For two hours? Very nice. Let's go have us a chat with Herr Busch.
(to Głowak)
Głowak, remember about the tailors.
Geniek exits with the Ukrainian. Głowak writes down the numbers and exits with the card.

FRYDERYK: It would be an atrocity if that fool were sent to his death. He was definitely not escaping. It's impossible.

JAN: Most likely.

---

[13] "Yes, I understand. I was in the latrine."
[14] "Where did you go?"

FRYDERYK: But he'll stand on that circumstantial evidence before Busch.

JAN: —Who understands no human tongue.

FRYDERYK: Why didn't they take me there as *Dolmetscher*.

JAN: Because the trial will last only a few minutes and without any pertinent questions.

FRYDERYK: It's unconscionable that we go along with this madness.

JAN: Yes and no. Geniek goes along because he knows that action might save many lives.

FRYDERYK: How can you say that? Everybody's life is valuable.

JAN *(with a bitter smile)*: Protest, then. The road's open. We'll have two corpses instead of one.

FRYDERYK: Maybe we should pressure Geniek?

JAN: How? He's already talking to Busch.

FRYDERYK: This is crazy. There has to be some solution.

JAN: I figured one out long ago.

FRYDERYK: What is it?

JAN: Stop thinking about it.

FRYDERYK: But it's enough to drive one mad!

JAN: Forgive me, Fryderyk, but you remind me of a man I knew in Buchenwald. He had a stomach disorder, *Durchfall*, diarrhea in other words. I gave him a lot of opium, as much I could, somewhere around a hundred drops. Not only did he not stop shitting, but he began vomitting twice as much. And I couldn't give him anything more for the diarrhea because he died that very same day. It's a bit like that with you.

FRYDERYK: There's this novella of Jensen's about his visit to a music hall in Mexico: a charming tropical evening, gorgeous chorus girls, one exhilarating number after another, a sense of having died and gone to heaven. But something prevents him from crossing the threshold. The author is sitting in the twentieth row, while in the first sits somebody tall and completely bald. If it's possible to speak of ideal baldness, the author maintains that this one was precisely ideal, like a sphere, a billiard ball. And the light thrown onto the stage from somewhere in the back, reflected off that perfect orb and radiated, hurting Jensen's sight. After some consideration, Jensen devises a plan to get rid of the painful glare. He takes out his revolver and shoots at the baldness, which spatters and no longer interferes with his immersing himself in the wonderful atmosphere of the production. Tell me, how, in this situation, we could dream up an equally simple solution to this problem that is choking us to death?

JAN: A solution like that is possible only in a story, and, at that, as long as the author isn't seeking a realistic way out of the situation. *Geniek and Czesiek run in.*

GENIEK: *Heil Hitler! Seig Heil!* It's over. Kaput. Done, you could say. The *Lagerschutze* are getting fifty cigarettes each from Fatso for their loyalty and cooperation. That's the end of it.

FRYDERYK: And what about the Ukrainian?

GENIEK: That cocksucker is going to be made into marmalade. I had barely pushed that half-wit into the room when Fatso jumped up. At me. Dancing around in a fit of fury. I thought that tub of lard was going to kill me. Revolver in one hand, whip in the other. And me holding nothing but my dick. I tell him that the *Lagerschutze* had caught one of the escapees who was still within the environs of the Lager. Apparently he hadn't yet managed to get across the wires and was hiding, waiting for the opportunity to do so. And Fatso instantly went like a pregnant cat at the Lagerschutz. I had to pull him off. It wasn't that one, I said, but this one. And I'd scarcely managed to point and that fool of a Ukrainian was already lying on the ground. How he beat him! Immediately. With his hands, feet, leash, whip, revolver. Unbelievable. Such agility in that heap of flesh! But the *Lagerleitung* is totally in the clear. Pure as a teardrop. So far, we've done more than the SS.

CZESIEK: F-fatso unburdened himself. T-tomorrow, he'll be as lyrical as a lover after l-losing his f-fiancee. Crepe on his arm, and a mandolin on his bulbous belly. Brum. brum, brum, brum. "I'll plant dill on your grave."

GENIEK: And who made all of this happen? Me!
He sits in the chair and puts his feet on the table.
—you could say the God and ruler of this here Lager. Just imagine: the Lagerschutze—who were sleeping—will receive fifty cigarettes a piece. This is the old guard. Pipel, grub!
He beats on the table with his feet.

PIPEL (O.S.): What should I serve?

GENIEK: Roasted flesh and coffee. And hurry it up before I rip you limb from limb.

PIPEL: Wait. I'll heat it up.

GENIEK: What else? Where are the tailors? I have to lay into their sorry asses.

JAN: They'll be right here. Głowak's gone to fetch them. They have to be dragged out of their bunks.

GENIEK *(dreamily)*: You could say I gave them the peelings. And they helped me do so. That guard who didn't want to get down from his tower, even though he'd learned about the escape, is a piece of work all right. And Fatso had an even better experience. When he ordered the chase, he met an SS and suggested he join the group. To which the SS replies that his shift is over and he has to rest. You get it? I thought that Fatso was going to have a stroke. And you know what he finally does? He makes the SS men take their coats off so they'd be more comfortable chasing the escapees. And the stupid fuckers went off without their coats, shivering from the cold.

ERNEST: They'll warm up.

GENIEK: But they won't be able to squat down anywhere along the road and take a nap. This way, those old geezers will have to tramp around the whole night long.

CZESIEK: Stop shitting around. Did he make them take them off? *Pipel enters, places food on the table, and exits.*

JĘDRZEJ *(entering as Pipel leaves)*: So how many stiffs do we have? The coffin's waiting.

GENIEK: One so far. Still warm, straight off the grill.

JĘDRZEJ: A clear weakening of the spirit on the part of the Germans. For a dog, a single Haeftling? That's cheap. In Auschwitz, for kicking the Lagerfuehrer's bitch, ten prisoners were shot. Those were the good old days.
Jędrzej climbs onto the bunk.

GENIEK *(eating and drinking voraciously)*: Where the hell's Głowak with those tailors?

JĘDRZEJ *(lying down on the bunk)*: You're going to talk to the tailors?

GENIEK: I have to find out where the escapees got civilian clothes.

JĘDRZEJ *(jumps down from the bunk)*: Ah, that's very good news. I was just wondering what to do with my time.
He reaches under the mattress, pulls out leather gloves and puts them on. He crosses near the door and sits, fidgeting.

CZESIEK *(looking at Jędrzej)*: Th-that young man can quite clearly distinguish between a rumbling stomach and a bowel disorder.

Czesiek pretends he's going to stroke Jędrzej's chin.

JĘDRZEJ: Back the fuck off! Wash your hands first, you Kaliskan yahoo.

CZESIEK: L-l-lay off Kaliska, or I'll cut you down to size. I swear.

JĘDRZEJ: Come on ahead! If you've got the balls.

CZESIEK: A-a-asshole. Go to the *Revier*. Th-they'll give you a shot of phenol.

JĘDRZEJ: Watch your mouth! I'm one of those that did the giving.

CZESIEK: Of c-course, creator of angels, of course. But I don't need artificial stimuli, oh former Minister of the Academy of the Quick Death.

JĘDRZEJ: It's a calming drug.

CZESIEK: A-and do you know who first said good-night? I'm trying to compile some statistical data.

JĘDRZEJ: About who shat all over himself, you lame-brained motherfucker?

GENIEK: All right! Enough! Come, gentlemen. Let's drink. To the health of my fiancee, a whore from Zielna Street. She was a good girl; let her work come easily. I'll bet Głowak says *memento mori* after each glass.

CZESIEK: A v-very nice habit, especially in the camp.

FRYDERYK *(sarcastically)*: What an imaginative conversation among professional pimps.

GENIEK: It appears we need to remind the lanky old, not-too-clever gentleman of *memento mori*. Drink up, my friends. When the moonshine tickles one's throat, one—
(loudly smacks his lips)

—gets shivers down his spine!
The bottle passes from hand to hand. Everybody drinks except Fryderyk and Jan.

GENIEK: And where the fuck is Głowak?
Głowak enters.

GŁOWAK: I brought the tailors. I had to round them up from the Blocks.

GENIEK *(with a pathetic gesture)*: We send you, Hermes.
(changes his tone)
You're an ass, Głowak, and, as opposed to a pig's ass, we can't make a ham sandwich out of you. Bring them here.

GŁOWAK *(leaning out the door)*: Come in.
Four tailors enter and stand by the door.

JAN: It seems things have cleared up. I still have three hours; I'm going to get some sleep. I suggest you do the same, Fryderyk.

FRYDERYK: If only I could. That damned *Schreibstube* operates twenty-four hours a day on my bed.
Jan exits.
During Jan and Fryderyk's conversation, Jędrzej goes up to the tailors, strokes them on the face, offers them cigarettes, and says something soothing to them.

GENIEK *(taking a swig of moonshine; to the tailors)*: So, boys, you know me and you know I'm a prick, right? And you know I know how to dish it out. So then, which of you gave the escapees civilian clothes?
The tailors are silent.

GENIEK: I know everything. Trading was good, but now you have to pay up. Start talking. You'll never guess who ratted you out. And if I get pissed . . . Sanin, you first.

SANIN *(in a Russian accent)*: I sold nothing.

GENIEK: I know that already. I want to know who did.

SANIN: I don't know.

GENIEK (*feigning anger*): What!? You limp-dicked, syphilitic pile of dog shit! What was it you told me today at noontime, scumbag? Who was it who came and ratted out his friends?
(*to the others*)
This is how it works when you do stupid shit . . .
(*to Sanin*)
So, you'll talk, you scaly cunt. Siberian sack of shit. Or do I have to break your fucking jaw?

SANIN (*mutters*): *Charasho ja etowo nie znaju.*[15]

GENIEK: So, asshole, tell me what you DO know.

SANIN: *Prodawal*[16] Markowski.

MARKOWSKI: I did not.

GENIEK: Jędrzej!

JĘDRZEJ (*slowly gets up from his chair*): When one can't deal politely with you, Markowski—
(*suddenly strikes Markowski in the teeth*)
—one has to show you what Lager means.

MARKOWSKI (*instinctively covers his face with his hands*): I did not sell clothes.

JĘDRZEJ (*shrilly; stammering*): Arms up! Raise your arms, or I'll kick you in the fucking nuts.
Markowski leans back; Jędrzej kicks him in the groin. Markowski doubles over.

---

[15] "Please I don't know who."
[16] "sold"

JĘDRZEJ: Stand up straight and keep your arms up, or I'll kick you again.
Jędrzej hits him on his lowered head with his knee.

GENIEK: Markowski, did you sell clothing?
Markowski shakes his head and wipes his bloodied mouth.

GENIEK: Jędrzej!

JĘDRZEJ: You're one tough motherfucker, but the routine of the Lager will change that. You're going to die today, ginger weenie, and Mommy is going to cry all over her little Benjamin, her poor little darling sweetie with violets in his hair. Spit it out, goddammit!! Did you sell civilian clothing?
Markowski shakes his head.

JĘDRZEJ: No, petunia? *Pasmotrim makolagwo,*[17] *Haeftling* shit, cocksucking crackpot cummed on by cows . . .
He hits Markowski in the chest and then in the groin. Markowski falls to the ground; Jędrzej kicks him.

JĘDRZEJ: Get up, you fucking pussy! You know how to take payments but can't stand on your own two feet?
Markowski slowly rises.

JĘDRZEJ: Arms up! Get your arms up, goddammit!!
Again he kicks Markowski in the groin; Markowski falls.

JĘDRZEJ: You're not fooling me with this shit. You're going to have to pay for the company you keep. Get up, you prick; otherwise, I'm going to kick your balls from here to December!
Markowski gets up and kneels, with his hands on the floor. Blood pours down his face. He struggles to his feet.

GENIEK: Markowski, did you sell clothing without stripes?

---

[17] "tailor songbird"

MARKOWSKI (*stubbornly shakes his head; tears in his eyes*):
Mama . . .

JĘDRZEJ: He's gone back home. The sonofabitch is calling for his mommy. Are you finally going to barf up the food you took for the clothes you sold? Raise your arms! Higher! Higher!
He hits Markowski in the groin again. Markowski falls to the ground unconscious.

JĘDRZEJ: Get up!
(kicks Markowski)
Get up, you thief, or I'll finish you off right now!
He drinks slowly, threatening the fallen Markowski with his fists.

GENIEK (*to the tailors*): Take him out and don't let this happen again. Next time, I'll take care of you myself.
The tailors exit carrying Markowski, whom Jędrzej sadistically kicks time and again.

CZESIEK (*sniggers*): T-t-to be continued. I c-c-can just imagine how Sanin is going to show his swollen face to the Lager. The t-tailors will beat the sh-shit out of him.

GENIEK (*indifferently*): Let them beat him to death, for all I care. It'll be a lesson to the others.
(stretches)
Well, this was a nice piece of work, *fertig*, wouldn't you say? And now—
(imitates the bubbling of liquid poured from a bottle)
—a little moonshine! Which of you gentle knights wishes to sit at this round table which is as sharp-edged as a muzulman's corpse before the turns of the crematorium?
He passes around the bottle of moonshine.

FRYDERYK: Not so much a table with sharp edges, as a table edged with sharpsters.

GENIEK: No one here is playing tricks. Everything's in keeping with the principles of the Lager: If you kick ass, you will last.

FRYDERYK: Lager principles: the killing of Poles by Poles.

GENIEK: Gentle, kindhearted Fryderyk, I advise you not to meddle in things that do not concern you.

FRYDERYK (*outraged*): These are my concerns. I, like you, am responsible for what goes on here.

GENIEK: Responsible, oh millionaire? What can YOU be responsible for, you who are kept by me, the lord, the God, of this Lager?

FRYDERYK: For seeing what goes on here and not protesting.

GENIEK: Oh, protest, protest . . .

JĘDRZEJ: Uncle has the right to defend his position. We are cultured people, officers for the most part. Not me, though, on account of my age . . .

FRYDERYK: Don't interrupt, puppy. I swear that what has happened here is a crime. It out-Hitlers Hitler. You've become Gestapo like those on the other side of the wires. You are unworthy of the name Poles. And if there ARE any officers among you, I swear, you are not worthy of the title. I swear the future Poland will be ashamed of you and will disavow you, and your rejection of all human feeling. I swear that I look at everything that goes on here and see Nazi barbarism magnified by Slavic thoughtlessness; I see that you are people who, in a normal society, would be hanged from the highest branch.

GENIEK: Is that all, old man?

FRYDERYK: I swear that all of your impulses, aimed at the saving of the lives of many people, or so you say, lead to the nightmare of everybody being murdered by everybody else. That your cooperating with the SS is a betrayal of your country. That you are hangmen and salesmen for whom nothing is sacred, neither God nor honor nor your homeland . . .

GENIEK (*sneering*): You are obviously right. What else do you wish to swear?

FRYDERYK (*increasingly animated*): If I manage to survive the Lager and return to Poland, I will use all possible means and influences at my disposal to reveal you, who will be regarded as national martyrs in your true light: highwaymen and ruffians, murderers and renegades. I swear that I will do everything to hold you responsible for the death of that Ukrainian, for beating Markowski bloody, for starving people, for doing nothing when you could have helped, for the filth, for the lice, for the law of the fist and stick as the only measure in camp conditions.

GENIEK: You won't do that, you old goat fuck . . .

FRYDERYK: I will. Otherwise, this blood will follow me and cry out for justice. You need to be dragged before a court of law. You need to be cauterized with iron, like a cyst. You need to realize that you are the outcasts of society for whom the only recourse is the isolation ward in an insane asylum!!

GENIEK: You won't do that, old man, because when I get you . . .

FRYDERYK: I'm not afraid of your threats . . .

GENIEK: I don't threaten; I strike!
Geniek leaps off the chair and punches Fryderyk in the chest. When Fryderyk covers himself, Geniek holds him down with his left hand and gives him a severe blow to the stomach. Fryderyk falls like a sack to the ground.

GENIEK: OK. *Fertig* with him. Sonofabitch!! I nearly fucked myself up listening to that idiot. Lay him down on the bunk; he'll get over it by tomorrow. What? He expected me to lay down my head instead of that Ukrainian half-idiot? A few blows to Markowski's nose, who was as good as dead anyway? Christ! Sanin could have finished him off at the gate and he's got his balls in an uproar?! I snag God knows what all from the SS storerooms and I don't have the right to eat what I feel like? I starve people?! I gave him a place to lie in the *Stube*; he enjoyed the same food I did, didn't work a lick. He's got bats in his fucking belfry, that one. A fucking rat pissed in his porridge. Let's drink. *Szulim*!

The bottle circulates.

During Geniek's monologue, Czesiek and Głowak move the Schreibstube's plank and put the unconscious Fryderyk on the bunk.

CZESIEK: It's o-obvious that that fuck didn't go through Auschwitz.

GENIEK: Never mind Auschwitz. He's gone through nothing. I put my arms around him as soon as he came to Buchenwald. I brought him here. Fed him, gave him drink, good clothes. And this is the gratitude I get. Ungrateful old faggot. So, he's going to squeal like a fucking pig when they liberate us? No. Uh-uh. I'll be the one to make him squeal.

JĘDRZEJ: In Auschwitz, when you saw someone behaving like a jackass, you knew immediately he was a professor or a clerk, an artist or a salesman.

GENIEK: And if someone fucked up a piece of bread, you'd know immediately he'd been a judge or a lawyer.

CZESIEK: All of th-them became muzulmen in a flash. And they had the best work on the *Holzhof* kommando . . .

ERNEST: I remember the first Christmas. I had already been there six months, which was a very long time under those conditions. An enormous Christmas tree full of candles and ornaments was lit up on the *Appellplatz*. The *Appell* was late. The Christmas tree shone like a meteor in the darkness. There was heavy snow. We were already standing in rows. Only the Holzhof was missing. They were late that day. At last, they came in through the gate, out of the darkness like ghosts. Thin; dry as skeletons. An eerie sight. Some were being led by their companions and walked like wooden dolls. The Kommando had with it a cart drawn by stronger *Haeftlingen* and on it were that day's corpses. They started unloading the bodies out of the cart and placing them, as though in mockery, beneath the enormous Christmas tree lit up from top to bottom. That heap of frozen corpses was a Christmas Eve gift from the Lager Kommando to the *Haeftlingen*. That's what the intelligentsia Kommando looked like: living corpses, dancing skeletons.

CZESIEK: Oh, you poor, over-sensitive little girl. The sight of dead muzulmen offends you. And to live for a while in the same bed as a corpse isn't a favor? I was lying half-dead in the *Revier* with typhus, and since there weren't enough bunks, they put two of us in one. Unfortunately, I got a half-dead guy with Durchfall, which streamed out of him every few minutes. So there I lay, in a sauce of diarrhea waiting for the gas . . . for death . . . for who knows what. *Arbeit Macht Frei.* But the guy with Durchfall finished himself off before me. He suddenly became cold, completely drenching me. So I called to the *Pfleger* who was walking by, "Take him away from me, he's already cold." "Wait, sonofabitch," he said. "In a couple of hours you'll both be out of here." And with those words of comfort, he walked off. I lay belly-to-back with a cadaver for nearly twenty-four hours.

GENIEK: Want a drink?
(He pours for them.)
The old-timers know what moonshine is.
They all drink.
Let me tell you what happened to Romek. You know him, the show-off from the Lager orchestra, always up for a drink. One night, Romek comes up to me and says, "I've got some vodka." There were maybe two, maybe three liters of it—enough for the four of us: Romek, me, Fryc, and Kurt, the one with the red triangle. We take a swig, goes down like glycerine. But Romek, after we'd drunk, went crazy. "Not enough," he says. "Wait." Then he vanishes and about a quarter of an hour later he's back with a couple of bottles of authentic denatured alcohol. No problem. We drink that, too. The inside of my head went black. I remember that we lay down on the bunks and Romek kept on drinking with somebody. Then strange things started to happen. First, Romek sang, then started to vomit uncontrollably. He vomited like Niagara, in violet, pink, every damn color. Then he began begging us to save him. And the more he begged, the more we laughed. "Vomit,

buddy, vomit. Empty yourself out," we advised him. "Maybe you'd like a little more denatured alcohol?" Then I fell asleep. I wake up in the morning, and because it was some big holiday or other, there was no work and everyone else was asleep. I look down—I was on an upper bunk—and a foot is sticking out from under a blanket. I look. Romek should be lying there. And the foot is neither blue nor green. So I get up and go to Romek. And his eyes are glassy and he's staring in the distance. "Romek," I say. But he's as stiff and cold as an English lord. He'd simply croaked in the night while we were asleep.

CZESIEK: I was in Birkenau when they brought the Dutch in to be gassed. In luxuriously appointed Pullmans, entire trains of well-fed plantation owners, bankers, and *Geschefte*. Stout, cultured gentlemen and pleasant ladies. All of them asked us where the allotments and fields in which they were to work were. And we looked at them, at their possessions, their trunks and suitcases, cosmetic bags, at their gold, some of it ostentatiously worn, and, above all, at their children. Gorgeous, well-dressed European children without a trace of Semitism. Smiling to everybody and everything. And then came "*Los . . . Los.*" The men were separated from the women. The men went to the gas first, and then the women and children. At one point, when the women were waiting their turn, a teeny, maybe four-year-old child ran off from the group destined for the gas and went into the Lager. I tell you, I've never seen anything as beautiful as this little girl. And beautifully dressed in some kind of shimmering satin. I would have been afraid to touch it. You know how it was with the residential Blocks. They stood not far off. And that little girl wandered into such a Block, empty, of course. The Block Elder, a professional criminal, took her by the hand, led her into his quarters and offered her chocolate and candy from Canada. He played with her for an hour, and then took her back to the collection point. But the women weren't there any longer. They'd all gone to the gas. It was empty. The child roamed among the wires, lonely and hapless. One of the SS men working near the crematorium sees this. "And you," he says, "Where have you got to?" And he takes that beautiful child, that golden-haired spring, a teeny princess from Dulac's fairy tales and bashes her head against the crematorium wall. I had seen things unheard of, things that would freeze the blood in your veins, but one more moment and I would have jumped at that bastard's throat. That spineless sonofabitch. I felt overcome and I grit my teeth like a wild dog. I thought I had gone mad. Fortunately, it passed. But to this very day . . . even if I were to forgive them for myself, my family, the lost years . . . I will never forgive them that one thing. When I remember that moment, blood rushes to my head. That four-year-old spring . . .

GENIEK: OK. *Kurwa wasza mac.* Why have you all gone mawkish all of a sudden? Huh? Heads high, gentlemen; otherwise, we'll scrub the tomb with our asses. It happened; it's over. Like a toothache. Some things bother me, too. Hell, I carried Natasha from the *Celt* Lager with my own hands to the gas chamber. You all knew her. And I'm alive. And I fuck the Germans in the eye with a broom handle. At the day of reckoning, we'll settle accounts. I ain't cheap. Drink up, boys. You wore yourselves out today. To a hair, you could say. But I sure got to him, didn't I?

JĘDRZEJ: Who? Fatso?

GENIEK: No. The chessman. You're so naive that you probably still believe in angels and storks. Why did they lock you up?

JĘDRZEJ: They had their reasons.

GENIEK: Drink up, friends. I'm the *Lageraeltester* and I look out for my boys.

JĘDRZEJ: I always said that Geniek was stand-up. Such a guy . . . *He makes a characteristic gesture with his hand.*

GENIEK: I am. But you, shithead, have a short reach and a weak right hand.
Geniek rolls a cigarette and pushes the tobacco to the others. At the same time, Jędrzej pulls the gold bridge out of Geniek's pocket, looks at it a moment, tests its value with his teeth, and then hides it in his pocket. The others see this, but say nothing.

JĘDRZEJ: So, you're saying I've got a short reach, huh? It gets me what I need, I reckon.

He crawls onto the bunk and lies down and instantly falls asleep.

GENIEK *(to Czesiek)*: Drink, O vaunted Nazi propagandist for the gutter press, stuck in the eye with an umbrella. *Szulim!* It's finished now.

(hands him the bottle)

There'll be moonshine; I've arranged everything . . .

(starts singing, accompanied by Czesiek)

Organize, from the gallows, if only string;
Organize, if you haven't become a prick.
Organize; stuff it all in your drawers,
For tomorrow we might swing on high, sonofabitch!
Organize, from Canada bags of loot.
Organize, before an SS man says to you "pas"—
Organize girls, diamonds, and fat
In Berlin or in Amsterdam.

Blackout (End of Act Two)

Act III

The Lageraeltester's room as in the first act. Four-thirty in the morning.
The window is covered with rags. The electric light is on. An enormous
mess everywhere. Offstage, sounds of people getting up to go to work;
shouts about the distribution of food float in. Fryderyk is lying in an
awkward position, fully dressed, on his bunk. Jędrzej and Geniek are
sleeping on the two bunks opposite. Jan enters cautiously, looks around,
and goes to Fryderyk.

JAN: Fryderyk!
Fryderyk doesn't move.

JAN: Fryderyk!
(gently touching him)
Wake up! What's the matter with you?
Fryderyk tries to lift his head.

JAN: Fryderyk, what's wrong?

FRYDERYK *(whispers)*: Fetch a doctor. Please. I'm bad, my
heart . . .

JAN: The doctors are still asleep. First, let's make you more
comfortable. What happened?

FRYDERYK: It happened . . .

JAN: What, Fryderyk?

FRYDERYK *(still in a whisper)*: . . . that he hit me.

JAN: Who?

FRYDERYK: Geniek.

JAN: Was he drunk?

FRYDERYK *(with effort)*: No. I threatened him with consequences. After the war . . .

JAN: Oh. I see.

FRYDERYK: Open the window . . . some air . . .
Jan gets on the bunk and takes the curtain off the window. Light of early dawn enters the room. Jan undoes Fryderyk's prison jacket, dampens a towel, and places it on his heart. Then he strokes his hair.

FRYDERYK *(barely audible)*: Such an end . . .

JAN: Come now, Fryderyk.

FRYDERYK: . . . this journey across the world. I'm dying.

JAN: We'll go to Warsaw together again. Right now you need to lie still and get some rest.

FRYDERYK: No.

JAN: You must.

FRYDERYK *(searching)*: And I so much wanted to hear the murmur of a young forest again. To hear the wind blowing . . . f ree . . . on a hill . . . between the branches of the trees. I so much wanted. . . . This pounding in my head! A bell clanging. If only it were all in Poland. . . . This, this pain . . . this death.

JAN: Be still now. Don't tire yourself.

FRYDERYK *(bitterly)*: They tormented me. Poles on a Pole. Kicked like a dog, an old fool who believed in the human heart and its wisdom . . .

JAN *(sadly)*: Heart in the Lager . . .

FRYDERYK *(agitated, barely conscious)*: But when you return to Poland, tell everyone that the old fool died because he steadfastly believed in the sanctity of man. Tell them that he didn't compromise himself, he who once played Lear and Hamlet and Judas and Heracles. Prometheus . . . and Tartuffe . . .

JAN: I will.

FRYDERYK: Look after yourself.
A long moment of silence. Jan sits deep in thought beside Fryderyk. The morning birds sing.

FRYDERYK: Do you hear the birds? They're free. The joy of spring is in their voices. The singers of the sky. Like in Poland.
Fryderyk passes out.

JAN: Fryderyk!
Jan dampens Fryderyk's forehead with a towel.

FRYDERYK *(conscious again, faintly)*: The sky . . . azure . . . like in Poland. A drop of Polish water would heal me. And here a *Haeftling's* pit . . . without four bits of wood . . . naked . . .

JAN: Stop. Don't fill your head with these thoughts.

FRYDERYK: But it bothers me . . . that there won't even be a coffin . . .
Fryderyk breathes ever more quietly.

JAN *(anxiously)*: I'm going for a doctor.

FRYDERYK: Don't leave. It's hard for me. A mist before my eyes . . .
(suddenly, in a resounding voice, almost rising from the bunk)
Is it you?
Jan leans helplessly over him.

FRYDERYK *(with fervor)*: Yes, me. A fool . . . I fought . . .
(words fading)

The gardens were mine . . . and the flowers . . .
Jan brushes Fryderyk's hair from his forehead. A ray of light bursts through the gaps in the wooden wall and settles on the face of the old actor, lending it dignity and beauty.

JAN: Fryderyk . . .

FRYDERYK *(gazing off)*: Always light. . . . A sunny world . . .
Jan hurries out of the room.

FRYDERYK *(stirring, jolting)*: Take that dog . . . Wilhelm! Wilhelm!
(more quietly)
Open your eyes . . . to the ever more radiant . . .
(still more quietly)
. . . glow.
He falls silent and still. Jan returns with the doctor in tow. They approach Fryderyk. The doctor checks Fryderyk's pulse, then shakes his hands.

DOCTOR: His pulse is fading. A matter of hours . . . perhaps minutes.

JAN: Can nothing be done?

DOCTOR *(shaking his head)*: In these conditions . . .
The doctor pulls back Fryderyk's sleeve and gives him an injection. Fryderyk stirs and looks at the doctor with wide-open eyes.

FRYDERYK *(in a whisper)*: It's the end, Stefan . . .

DOCTOR: Take heart, old Lear.

FRYDERYK: Oh, I have it.
(laboring to speak, rasping)
But why here, on foreign soil, does death meet up with me? It's bitter. Just to have a wisp of our sky . . . the murmur of the wind. And some soft white curtains fluttering in a room filled with sunlight. If only a bird from there would sing.

DOCTOR: Easy, old Lear. You'll hurt yourself.

FRYDERYK: Polish hands. Polish! As so many times,
always . . . terrible hands. Forks and wheels . . . and the axes of
hatred. The heart bleeds . . .

JAN: Fryderyk, don't work yourself up. We'll take you to the *Revier*.

FRYDERYK *(following a train of thought)*: I have nothing, Jan,
nothing that is mine. They took everything. Grabbed the smallest
souvenir and destroyed it. Dropped me naked into the Lager.
And now they'll put me out naked . . . into the earth. Jan, I am
not afraid . . . but the poverty of this leave-taking is terrible, this
misery . . . this ugliness. . . . If only a flower from those fields . . .
*Jan looks around. He searches and in a corner finds the dried flowers
sent to Górecki. He places the bouquet in Fryderyk's hand. Fryderyk
squeezes his fingers tight around the dry stems.*

FRYDERYK: At my burial throw these flowers into the grave.
Remember . . .
Jan nods his head.

FRYDERYK *(whispering to himself)*: Flowers, tiny flowers with sweet
names and glances . . . infinite joy . . .
(obviously struggling)
Jan . . .
*Jan pulls up a stool and sits as close to Fryderyk as possible, leaning
over him.*

FRYDERYK: Don't laugh. You know the beginning of *Pan
Tadeusz* . . . Say it to me. It's alive . . . like these flowers.

JAN *(quietly)*
Lithuania, my homeland! You are like good health:
How much you should be prized, only he knows
Who has lost you. Today, I see and describe you
In all your splendor because I yearn for you so.
Holy Virgin, who protects bright Częstochowa

And sparkles in Ostra Brama! You, who shield
The castled town of Nowogrodek and its loyal people—
As you miraculously restored me, a child, to health—
(When my weeping mother entrusted me
Unto your care, I opened a lifeless eyelid
And instantly was able to walk to Your shrine's door
To thank God for my life restored)—,
So will you return us to our native land.
In the meantime, carry my yearning heart
To those wooded hillocks, the green meadows
Stretching broad along the azure Niemen River,
To the fields, painted with all kinds of grain,
Made golden by wheat, and silver by rye,
With amber mustards and buckwheat white as snow,
Where with a maidenly blush clover glows.
And all of this girdled by
A band of green like a ribbon—
On which, here and there, quiet pear trees squat.
Fryderyk closes his eyes. His face suddenly drops. Then his eyelids half
open and he remains like that. Jan is silent. He leans over Fryderyk
and delicately closes his eyes. A moment of great silence.

DOCTOR: He's dead.

JAN: An old child with pure impulses. A naive old actor with a
gentle heart. Gone. People like that always die too soon.

DOCTOR: What happened? He was healthy yesterday.

JAN (*bitterly*): He was. Pitchforks stabbed him, hooks pierced his
brain, heavy wheels broke his spine. An old issue, an old case.
Poland. Is there anywhere that beauty is hated as much as we hate
it? Dark forces operate within us, and our hatred erupts into death
and dissolution. And what are we in the end? A nation of iron fists
and empty heads.

DOCTOR: That's bitterness talking.

JAN: Yes, it is. Because people like that should be heeded. People
like him are the true flags of a nation, the keepers of the West's

eternal flame. Those funny, stubborn, useless fantasists whose eyes ought to be shielded from the sight of blood. How are we going to approach our work after the war, having been murdered and murdering in turn? We've become irretrievably profane. And in the name of what? Some strange hatred of light, of beauty. What harm did that old doll, that past full of reminiscences, that scrap of a broken-down ship, full of romanticism and the charm of well-traveled roads to the sun, do to anyone? Who did old Lear ever harm? And yet, eternal depravity festers inside us. That old madman talking in rhyme could have lived and thrilled a new generation with a tale of theatrical tragedy. He could have lived that St. George of tin, that Don Quixote of the Lager. He could have lived. . . .

DOCTOR: The conditions in the camp—

JAN: —have nothing to do with it. Each of us harbors a need to destroy; the Lager simply gives it teeth. All the safeguards have failed. The human machine goes where it wants, and all its impulses, all its crazed desires are immediately unleashed. We hold no dignity, no respect for ourselves, no respect for others, no love of humanity. Deep down, we want others to be worse than we are. We pray for an even greater evil.

DOCTOR: You were in Auschwitz . . .

JAN: Don't get me wrong. I'm far from condemning anyone. You can justify everything by taking conditions into account. All of us have become more or less abnormal with terrible lesions on our bodies and souls: Nobody went through Auschwitz unscathed. But the damage wouldn't be so complete if we didn't have these impulses deep within us. Our lack of vision and substance takes vengeance on us. We allow ourselves to be conquered not only territorially but spiritually, personally. What's worse is that we take a platitude created in the heat of the moment and treat it as an irrefutable law. We lose perspective. Idolatry is in our nature: We don't know how to respect ourselves. Black fires burn inside us and we don't want to see them.
(after a moment)
There are no greater rounders than the Slavs. It's almost criminal.

DOCTOR: What's happened to you, Jan?

JAN: I feel sorry for that old madman. He stumbled in among us from Wonderland and lived like the embodiment of a medieval fairy tale nibbled at by rats and mildew, but with a charming gesture and a certain aesthetic grace. Yes, he'd become a bit addled, but with his enthusiasm he could still have done much for a nation that often seems like straw pretending to be gold.

DOCTOR: You're being unfair.

JAN: What love is fair? I have a right to speak ill of a country that tolerates only self-praise in greedy doses. There has to be some counterpoint. All creative urges are destroyed in us by this self-adoration. We can't afford the open-sea bravery of long voyages after phantoms with leaden horns. We're stay-at-homes wallowing in self-satisfaction, high priests bowing our heads to ourselves. Why do we still have the right to live? We are filled with a kind of military bravery, but not a cent's worth of human courage. And this lack of courage, together with the most treacherous mendacity, in moments free of drinking vodka and playing dirty tricks, crowing about personal heroism and martyrdom, killed that good, old child.

DOCTOR: Yes. Without doubt.
They both stand deep in thought. Suddenly, from the Block—

VOICES (O.S.) *(shouting)*: *Arbeitskommando antreten! Los! Los! Raus!* Out the door! Now! Now!! Assemble!

DOCTOR: I'll send the *Leichentraeger*.

JAN: Let me know about his burial. I'd like to throw those flowers into the grave for him.

DOCTOR: Of course.
The doctor exits. Jan approaches the sleeping Geniek.

JAN: They're calling an *Appell*. Get up; you have to go out.

GENIEK: Why?

JAN: I don't know. Lager custom.

GENIEK: Because someone shit himself?

JAN: As usual, you, you genius.

GENIEK: Geniuses don't shit.

JAN: Okay, then, pick another reason. But you have to get up.
Moira!

GENIEK: Why do you keep going on about those Jewish women?
This isn't Auschwitz.

JAN: Get out of bed, or I'll soak you.
*Geniek sits up on the bed, pale and semiconscious, his clothing
crumpled.*

GENIEK: What? It's day already?

JAN: My, my! Signs of life are already flashing through you.
Fryderyk has died.

GENIEK: Where?

JAN: Right here.

GENIEK: Go to the *Revier*, and tell them to organize a party three
days from now. Pipel! Shoes.
*Geniek collects himself quickly. Pipel enters with the polished shoes.
Geniek dresses and runs out of the room. Two Leichentraegers enter
with a stretcher. Jan goes to Fryderyk and takes the bouquet of dried
flowers out of his hand. The Leichentragers place Fryderyk's body on the
stretcher. Jędrzej stirs awake.*

JAN *(to one of the Leichentragers)*: Tell Stefan to arrange a party in
three days time.
*The Leichentrager nods. He and his partner carry Fryderyk's body out of
the room. Jan stands opposite the window gazing out.*

JĘDRZEJ: It's good that I ordered them to make a coffin yesterday. Two will be going to the *Kirchhof.* Amazing, a camp old-timer's intuition!
Jan doesn't respond and continues staring out the window.

JĘDRZEJ: You see angels there?

JAN *(without turning)*: Whom you won't have a chance to rob because they're all too far away. Get up, Sticky Fingers. Time to see to the people.

JĘDRZEJ *(lazily)*: I give them enough of my attention.

JAN *(unmoved)*: Not so much them as their wallets and false teeth.

JĘDRZEJ: I'll be damned! So you've been paying attention after all, eh, Jan?

JAN: Not me. I don't see a thing. Especially not your stupidities.

JĘDRZEJ: Not true, my friend. To have spent five years in the Lager and not have worked for even a single day is not the mark of a stupid man.

JAN: So you're a smart-ass created by the Lager. What'll happen to you when the Lagers disappear?

JĘDRZEJ: Don't threaten me, now, 'cause you'll just piss me off. Anyway, how can the Lagers disappear? Think about it . . .

JAN *(to himself, as though drawing a conclusion)*: Yes, well . . .

JĘDRZEJ: As long as there are Lagers, I'll be in them. It's good for me here.

JAN: You don't want to go free?

JĘDRZEJ: I'm not free here? Food, laundry, girls, gold. What more do I need? And all of it costs me nothing. And on top of that, I get to fleece a few people every day.

JAN: What about grass and sunshine, a flowing river, murmuring forest . . . a winding road and open space . . .

JĘDRZEJ: I have all of that.

JAN: —and Geniek beats the shit out of you every day.

JĘDRZEJ: Fuck Geniek! Up his ass! I'll settle the score with him. Never you fear.

JAN: I only fear that you might not live too long.

JĘDRZEJ: I know, my friend, I know. But I won't give you the satisfaction. People like me live for a long time.

JAN: People like you live a long time? In time, in time . . .

JĘDRZEJ: What are you muttering? With my skills I can easily become a minister in Poland, and Geniek chief of police.

JAN: Not trivial ambitions.

JĘDRZEJ: Not impossible ones, either. What can work in a ministry amount to when compared to organizing in a Lager? After such training? Hey, don't jerk me around, or I'll give you what-for!
Jedrezej crawls off the bunk and rolls a cigarette out of the tobacco Geniek left behind.

JĘDRZEJ *(shouting)*: Pipel!!
Pipel runs in.

JĘDRZEJ: How come no grub or drink, asswipe? You want to go work a spade?

PIPEL: Coming right up.
Pipel exits. Jędrzej examines a piece of gold from his pocket.

JĘDRZEJ *(deep in thought)*: You know that Fryderyk had something . . .

JAN: I know.

JĘDRZEJ: A few days ago I was looking in his jacket and found a gold signet ring.

JAN: You robbed Fryderyk?

JĘDRZEJ: No, I played hide-and-seek. And the following day I exchanged the signet ring for some vittles. Now, however, I have it again.
Głowak and enters and puts the Schreibstube table on Fryderyk's bed. He arranges files and papers on the table. Jan takes the paper he needs and exits.

GŁOWAK: The Kommandos have gone out.

JĘDRZEJ: What the fuck? Don't we know this already? Where's Geniek?

GŁOWAK: Talking to the *Lagerfuehrer*. That Ukrainian has to be moved to the *Revier*.

JĘDRZEJ: Did they beat him or shoot him?

GŁOWAK: He's all purple. But he's also got a big hole in his neck.

JĘDRZEJ: In other words, business as usual. Very nice.

GŁOWAK *(sadly)*: A crucifix would be useful now.

JĘDRZEJ *(waving his hand)*: Don't shit your panties. Ivan will see to it.
Jędrzej gets on the bunk. Geniek runs in.

GENIEK *(crowing triumphantly)*: Ah, ha, ha, ha, ha! What? You corpses aren't still sleeping, are you? Pus-infected maggots! Misery must be your mother! Pipel! Grub!

PIPEL *(offstage)*: On my way!

GENIEK: *Bloedeaeltester*!

CZESIEK *(offstage)*: Coming!
Czesiek enters.

GENIEK: What are we doing?

CZESIEK: St-stench.

GENIEK: In other words, a rubber.

CZESIEK: Can't fail.

GENIEK: But we don't have a fourth.

CZESIEK: Why not?

GENIEK: Fryderyk died.

CZESIEK: The man could never be taken seriously.

GENIEK: But who will you take?

CZESIEK: H-how about . . . Kazik?

GENIEK: Good. Get him. And Ernest.

CZESIEK *(leaning out the door)*: Ernest! Kazik!
Ernest and Kazik enter.

GENIEK: Let's play, gentlemen. Time's precious. Time is money.
And life is short.
Everyone sits down at the table.

KAZIK: What are we playing for?

GENIEK: For a mark. As usual. Okay?
The others nod.

ERNEST: Who's dealing?
Everyone takes a card.

GENIEK: I am. My house; I deal. Always.

KAZIK: A true man of principle.

GENIEK: What's that supposed to mean, asshole?

KAZIK: Principles are made to be broken.

GENIEK: No joking around, you prick. You're too young to be clever.
Geniek shuffles the cards, cuts them, and deals them.

GENIEK: I call spades.

CZESIEK: Pass.

ERNEST: Pass

KAZIK: Two clubs.

GENIEK: Pass.

CZESIEK: Pass.

ERNEST: Pass.

KAZIK: Play.
They play a rubber.

GENIEK: Read 'em and weep!

KAZIK: I have such wonderful luck. Whatever I play, I take it up the ass.

ERNEST *(looking at the cards on the table)*: What's that?

CZESIEK: W-what if I told you it's the *Moonlight Sonata*?

GENIEK: Tomato sauce with parmesan.

KAZIK: A bowel movement.

GENIEK: What? You don't have any diamonds?

ERNEST: I'll go beat my meat.
(singing "Ramona" under his breath)
"Phlegmon, stubborn flower of my legs . . ."

CZESIEK: Listen, Ernest. Komek is sick; maybe he should be moved to the new *Revier*.

ERNEST: We'll make up the beds and pack him in there.

JĘDRZEJ: What's the hurry, huh? I haven't ordered the coffin yet.

CZESIEK *(throwing his cards on the table)*: What do you say to that?

GENIEK: Pipel! Bring me some grub! Or I'll beat your face to a pulp!

JĘDRZEJ: Bring me some, too.

PIPEL (O.S.): Coming right up! I'm heating the coffee.

Blackout (THE END)

Concentration Camp Terms

Antreten	A line-up of prisoners.
Appell	Roll call.
Arbeitsdienstfuehrer	Work deployment leader (SS).
Arbeitseinsatz	Deployment of labor.
Arbeitszeit	Work time.
Aussenkommando	Unit of prisoners working outside the Camp.
Canada	The name of this country, seen as land of plenty, was synonymous in the camp with "riches." It was the term used for areas of the camp where possessions taken from new transports of prisoners were stored, and from which experienced old-timers "organized" alcohol, cigarettes, clothing, etc. for themselves.
Dolmetscher	Translator.
Gaertnerei	Horticulture.
Haeftling (-en)	Prisoner (-s).
Holzschuhe	Wooden clogs worn by the prisoners.
Kapo	Prisoner in charge of a work detail.

Kirchhof	Burial ground.
Kommando	Work detail.
Lager	The Camp.
Lageraeltester	Camp Elder, prisoner in charge of the Camp, chosen by and directly answerable to, the SS Commandant.
Lagerfuehrer	Camp Commandant (SS)
Lagerleitung	Higher-ranking prisoners with positions of responsibility and authority in the Camp.
Lagerschutz(-e)	Camp guards, prisoners.
Leichentraeger	Corpse carriers.
Muzulman	*lit.* Muslim. A totally depleted prisoner on the brink of death.
Organizing	Acquisition of means of survival from official areas of the Camp—kitchen, storage rooms, ramp. As opposed to "stealing" taking items from another prisoner.
Pfleger	Nurse.
Posten	Camp guards (SS).
Revier	Camp hospital.
Schreiber	Clerk.
Schneider	Tailor.
Schreibstube	Office.
Vorarbeiter	Foreman of a work unit, Kapo's assistant.
Zebrakleidung	Concentration camp striped uniforms.
Zugang(-e)	Newcomer (-s) to the Camp.

www.ingramcontent.com/pod-product-compliance
Lightning Source LLC
LaVergne TN
LVHW091225080426
835509LV00009B/1174